SPEECH

OF

HON. THOMAS CORWIN,

OF OHIO,

IN THE HOUSE OF REPRESENTATIVES,

JANUARY 23 AND 24, 1860.

Monday, January 23, 1860.

Mr. CORWIN said:

Mr. CLERK: I rise to inquire what is the subject under discussion at this time? [Laughter.]

The CLERK. The question before the House is the point of order raised by the gentleman from Iowa [Mr. CURTIS] on Thursday last.

Mr. CORWIN. Then the speech of the gentleman from Mississippi, [Mr. BARKSDALE,] to which we have listened with a good deal of interest, has been made, I understand, upon the point of order.

The gentleman from Mississippi wants to get rid of this cumbrous business, and I will say to him that the only way to accomplish it is by voting; and I say further to him, that if he should be elected, I will pledge him that the State of Ohio will not dissolve the Union on that account. Now, this is a very serious matter, though, at the same time, it so happens that almost every good or grave subject discussed by men will have something ludicrous about it. This farce which we have been enacting for seven weeks, very much to our amusement, is, as we hear it very frequently remarked, and sometimes much to the disturbance of some gentlemen here, beginning to be, in the minds of the people of this country, a serious matter. If every gentleman here who has a duty to discharge, and who was sent here to do the business of this great Republic, would put this matter to his conscience as he does other subjects which involve questions of conscientious duty, surely we would begin to think seriously what we have to do.

I know that there are some very plausible arguments—and to me they are difficult to get over—in favor of electing a Speaker of the House by the majority of votes of members. I was reminded the other day by one of my friends, resident in this city, with whom I have long had most agreeable and friendly intercourse—a gentleman in good standing with the present Administration, and therefore I do not wish to give his name, lest it might bring him into disrepute [laughter]—that there was something in the election of Speaker more than I had supposed; that in a certain event he might become President of the United States. I confess that puzzled me a little. It may be so; but I do not think it important that we should incorporate that idea into our purposes, as one of the contingencies that may arise. It is hardly possible that any two gentlemen who are or may be elected President and Vice President will be amiable enough to die for the benefit of the Speaker of this House. I do not know what God in his providence may have in store for us. Such a contingency has never happened, and therefore I think we should not give it a marked place in our consideration of the question of the Speakership of this House. Something has been said by the gentleman from Mississippi touching this very subject; and I, reserving my rights under such rules of order as we may hereafter establish, desire to say something on the general propositions that have been so ably presented to the House by the gentleman from Mississippi.

The gentleman read, as the bitterest drop in the cup, some paragraphs from the Helper book, advising that the free laboring population of the South, not holding slaves, shall abstain from communication with those who do own slaves. Now, I wish to ask gentlemen of the South what they suppose would be the result of placing this book in the hands of the non-slaveholding people of the South? The question would simply be submitted by those non-slaveholding men of the South to the whole State, whether slavery should be abolished or not; and if it should be determined to abolish slavery, would anybody have a right to complain of a State for abolishing slavery, more than to complain of her for adopting it? Gentlemen have greatly overrated the consequences of that little book. I know that they say, or have said, that it shows the disposition of the North to interfere with slavery in the South. How does it show that disposition? It was written, as everybody knows, by a man who had his citizenship or habitation in North Carolina until he left there to go to the city of New York. Who is to blame, then, if we may trace back effect to cause? You say that Mr. SEWARD made a speech in Rochester, some time in the year of grace 1858, and that from that came the invasion of Virginia, by twenty-three men, headed by John Brown.

Sir, if North Carolina had not brought up this man among her own slave institutions, we never should have had the Helper book. No Northern man has written such a book; and if he had written such a book, is it possible that any institution existing in a Christian and enlightened community like the South can be overthrown by a pamphlet? In a congregation of children of the same family, I should avoid a subject which might disturb our relations. I would not like to throw into the face of my brother one of his evil habits; nor would you, my friends.

Mr. Clerk, history will show that Mr. SEWARD, if he be the great leader of the Republican party—and I have almost given up all pretensions to their leadership since I have been loudly and positively repudiated by one side of the House, and some on this side have said pretty much the same thing—I say that Mr. SEWARD has never uttered a sentiment, and that one cannot be cited in all the extracts which have been quoted from his speeches or his arguments, more offensive to the South than Thomas Jefferson, the apostle of Democracy, did utter. I know that my friends from the South are too well acquainted with the history of that great man, not to know, as I know, that neither Mr. SEWARD, nor any other Republican—I except the Abolitionists, for they are not Republicans, but, on the contrary, generally hold the Republican party in utter scorn—I say that in Helper's book nothing is to be found, so far as I know, more offensive than utterances long since found in writings and speeches of the elder men of the South. George Washington himself always said while he lived that he should wish, if it were possible, to see slavery abolished in the United States. I know that Mr. SEWARD, whose election as President of the United States it is said will be the signal for civil war in this great Confederacy, has never said anything more offensive to the South than has been said by your ambassador whom you have lately commissioned to France, (Mr. Faulkner, of Virginia,) taking it for granted that the extracts which I have seen quoted from his speeches are true extracts.

The eloquent gentleman from Mississippi [Mr. BARKSDALE] is very much afraid of the establishment, by the gentleman from Massachusetts, [Mr. BURLINGAME,] of an anti-slavery Bible. Sir, that Bible is a book without which, in my judgment, no society can very well exist and hope to advance in morals or otherwise. And yet I warn gentlemen, North and South, that it is a book which it will not do for us to look to alone to guide us in the organization of political society of the present day. We find, in the historical parts of that book, brief sketches of the laws, usages, and doings, of the people of the Old World, which, if not read and pondered more carefully than such as we are apt to do, may lead to great errors in legislation in this age and country. We find there enacted very much such scenes, thousands and thousands of years ago, as we have been endeavoring to enact in this little sphere of ours—about a tenth part, I suppose, of this habitable globe—which, of itself, to the mind of Isaac Newton, or Herschell, or La Place, if they had not been born and lived here, would seem to be a very insignificant portion of the universe. And yet, one would suppose, from the debates we have had here, that we really believed the happiness of all worlds, and certainly of untold generations, depended upon the election of A or B, to stand up there in that chair, like a "woodpecker tapping a hollow beach tree." [Great laughter.] That tapping, sir, has been to us, so far, the only exhibition of power or influence belonging to that office, about which we have been in angry contest for the last six weeks. We become so accustomed to the sound, that we do not think we are in order unless we hear that tapping. We do not think we are in Congress unless somebody is calling us to order, accompanied, too, by that continuous ever-recurring tapping.

But, sir, I was referring to the allusion made by the gentleman from Mississippi to the gentleman from Massachusetts, and an "anti-slavery Bible." How is this, sir? One wants an anti-slavery Bible, and he is sure he has it in our present version. Another wants a pro-slavery Bible, and he is equally certain he has it in the same sacred book. Let each be content with his belief, and not interfere *here* with that of his brother; let us not dissolve the Union upon conflicting constructions of the Bible. I think it is certain that those patriarchs held slaves, and that they transmitted them to their children; but they did not make slaves of their own people; and some other things are very certain. This fugitive slave law that we hear so much about: I will not pretend to go into particulars, but I think it will appear that it, or a rule something like it, had its constructions and repeals in the Bible time.

I think that when the bondwoman Hagar left Abraham, with her master's consent, there being some disturbance in his domestic relations, [much laughter,] the boy Ishmael, not being the child of promise, and being in the habit of making impertinent remarks about the conduct of family affairs, [laughter,] was sent off with his mother into the wilderness, with a loaf of bread and a bottle of water. We are told that Hagar, being exhausted and famished by hunger, laid the boy down to die, and that the Angel of the Lord came there. If I remember aright, it is so written in that book. And what advice did he give to this bondwoman and her son? The Angel told this woman that she was in very bad circumstances, but not to be discouraged; to pick up the boy and hold him in her hands, for he would become a great filibuster. [Roars of laughter.] That is the English of what the

Angel said, when you use our present word for expressing the idea conveyed by the record of this remarkable historical fact. His hand would be against every man, and every man's hand would be against him. That declaration has been literally fulfilled in the progeny of that boy up to this very hour; and the only nation that has made any impression upon his posterity has been the French in Algiers. The French killed off these filibusters, until they have got them into some very imperfect kind of obedience. From the day that the Angel of God made that prophecy in reference to this slave boy, his progeny have gone on filibustering, fighting, and robbing. This good quality they have had, I believe, in all their history: if you broke their bread and tasted their salt, they would die by you. I would that some of our Southern friends would treat some of our Yankee gentlemen as well, when they go amongst them. [Laughter.] The Angel told this mother that she had better go back into slavery. If that Angel had been an agent of the underground railway, then this mother would have been advised to take herself and son off to Canada. [Laughter.]

So much for the historical fact. That very able man who was the father of that boy had another family; and they, in a generation or two after this, were sold into slavery, and so they remained, we are told, for four hundred and seventy years. At the end of that time, God abolished that servitude and repealed the fugitive slave law, very much to the dismay and astonishment of the pursuing masters, and greatly to the gratification of those owing labor and service to them. Then he allowed them to go home—to their Africa, or, to speak without figure, to the home of their fathers. That repeal of the Egyptian fugitive slave bill, on the shore of the Red sea, with all its incidents, is worthy of some notice now, and at all times. We hear much said of women taking part in politics now-a-days. Something very like it occurred on the occasion to which I refer. Just as the bubbling death-groan of the Egyptian host had risen to the surface of the sea, and was borne away upon the hot breath of the winds, a woman, a notable woman, then and there broke forth in a very remarkable triumphal song. Miriam, the sister of Aaron, with all the dark-eyed daughters of the fugitive Hebrew slaves, shouted out, "Sing ye to the Lord, for gloriously hath He triumphed; the horse and his rider hath He cast into the sea." That was their "Hail Columbia." Sir, that song of the prophetess has rung in my ears in day, and often in night time, too. In my dreams of the ultimate destiny of man, I have supposed it would ring in the the ears and agitate the souls of men, till the words "kings and subjects, rulers and ruled," should be lost in two words, "brothers—sisters."

Mr. Clerk, I warn my brethren from the North and my brethren from the South, that they will scarcely agree as to what are the general teachings of the Bible on this subject of slavery as practiced in our times. I think parts of that Book very clearly inculcate the doctrine, which in our republican form of government is held very sacred by us, that the laws of the country, as they were established, should be obeyed by all good citizens. Certainly, Christ and the Apostles taught that they did not come to overturn Governments, but to search into the wicked hearts of men, and subvert the kingdom of Satan therein. The gentleman from Massachusetts, [Mr. BURLINGAME,] I dare say, can find some authority satisfactory to him for his doctrine, and the gentleman from Mississippi, [Mr. BARKSDALE,] for his; but both should draw the true moral, as philosophical Christian historians would do, and agree that that Book teaches us one lesson, at least, which in substance is, that in a country like ours, where every man has an agency in the making of the laws, all should render to them obedience, until they shall be made better or be repealed. For unless the laws are generally obeyed, we will have nothing but anarchy organized, which cannot be a condition pleasing to Him who is the common Father of all men. Hence the Republican doctrine is, that the laws of the country ought to be obeyed. I assert that our Republican leaders, generals, colonels, majors, captains, corporals, and privates, all of them, are conservative; and that the Republican party is a law-abiding party; and whosoever believes the contrary, labors under great ignorance of that party and the men who compose it.

Mr. Clerk, I wish to look for one moment at some other facts found in the historical portion of the Bible, having a curious bearing, at least, on this question of negro slavery. We are told in that same Book that the people of the globe, except eight, were destroyed in a deluge. Noah and his family only were preserved. That old patriarch seems to have been remarkable for nothing, so far as I can find out, except for his strong faith in the word of God, and his remarkable nautical adventure. Noah had three sons, from whom have sprung all the people now upon the face of this globe. We are told by sacred, and I think pretty fully, too, by profane historians, that Japhet is the father of our race. We, then, are all children of that man. We have, it is true, to go far back to get at it. He is our original *propositus*. Shem is the father of the migratory, wandering Asiatic family. Ham, it is said, was the father of the negroes. This, I think it will be found, is shown by our accredited historical books. Some have wondered how it happened that Japhet, born of the same mother, son of the same father, should be a gentleman with features and complexion like you and myself; Shem, a yellow fellow, with high cheek bones; and Ham, a negro, with black face and crisp, curled hair. This difficulty is surmounted by one class of ethnologists by attributing the difference to climatic influences, in which I think there is great plausibility. Be this as it may, the relationship is the same. Japhet, it is agreed, had large acquisitiveness, and hence his superiority; and it may be said, with equal truth, that his children are not deficient in this capital virtue, for such it is held to be in our times by us in this model Republic. They also, it is said, have quick and powerful faculties for numerals; and regard in theory, as well as practice, the multiplication tables as the acme of human knowledge. But let us look at this family imbroglio. We are the sons of Japhet, and the negro is the son of Ham; we are the sons, respectively, of these two brothers; and consequently we, the sons of Japhet, are cousins to Cuffee, he being the son of our uncle Ham. I have often thought if the negro, as seems from this account of us to be probable, had really that relationship to us, that we certainly had not treated our cousin like a gentleman! [Renewed laughter.]

So you see there are some curious reflections belonging to the subject. But, short-sighted mortals as we are, all we can do now is to look at the black man as *he* is, and the white man as *he* is. One of your statesmen of the South, whom I have had the pleasure of knowing for a good many years—I allude to Mr. Stephens, of Georgia—in a recent speech, said that he was in favor of Mr. SEWARD's higher law, not exactly in its application, but he said, that if it be not better for the white man as well as the black man, that one should be master and the other the slave, they had no business with slavery, and should surrender it. I give the substance, but perhaps not the exact words. All who have read that gentleman's speech to the people of Georgia will know that I quote him fairly. That, I think, is the true philosophic ground upon which to put it. If it be better that the negro should stand in the relation of slave, better for all concerned, then slavery is right. If the converse be true, then slavery is wrong, and of course, if it be possible, should be peaceably abolished. Thus this vexed question is stated and submitted to the world by a living, leading Southern statesman. Let calm reason and fair discussion by those whom it concerns ascertain the truth. The path of duty is then made plain to all.

I am not now and here about argue for either side of the question thus generally propounded; but one thing I will say: it is not a good thing for white or black men to hold negroes as slaves in the State of Ohio, because we have tried it. We are sure it is better that the black slave should not be where the white man has to work by the side of him. It is better, we think, that the work of our State should be done by its white men. We have concluded, without any doubt, that wherever the white man *can live and work*, there, at least, no system of forced labor should exist. It has been ordained that man shall "earn his bread by the sweat of his brow." There are but very few men living on the face of the earth, if they live honestly, who are not compelled to do something, by head or hand, or both, for their own subsistence. For instance: in the whole fifteen Southern States there are only about four hundred thousand who own slaves.

Mr. KEITT, (in his seat.) Heads of families.

Mr. CORWIN. I was speaking of the heads of families. That may involve an interest of two millions of people. Let it be so. I am not particular about it. There are eight million white people at the South, are there not? I wish there were one hundred million, for I want the South to be strong. A great majority of the Southern people must labor at something, as I doubt not they do. They who own slaves are the exceptions to this old rule. I am not about to make any invidious or ungracious remarks on these two classes of people. I am free to admit, and happy to say, with truth, that, North and South, we are the most favored and the happiest people that ever lived in the tide of time, and I think the history of the world will prove it. But we will not allow ourselves to think so; we are like Mr. Brown in the farce—we will allow ourselves to be "excited!" As there is no hostile flag from any part of the globe to disturb the repose of our thirty millions of free people, we, of course—such is the frailty and unsatisfied nature of man—will find causes for fearful conflict, at least among ourselves. And yet I would under no circumstances vote to furnish men and means to carry on war abroad, merely for the sake of avoiding internal strife. I prefer what I am sure, if we are not a doomed people, is easy and practicable, to put our passions and party animosities under recognizance to keep the peace where we are.

Now, as to the reason, so often demanded on the other side of the House, why the people of the North would prohibit slavery in the Territories of the United States. I shall be prepared, I hope, to discuss this subject without excitement, fully, whenever it properly comes before us, after this House shall organize. But I cannot forbear a hasty view of the subject, even now. It is called for by the great misapprehension of gentlemen on the other side, and the denunciations, founded on that misapprehension, to which we have, up to this time, listened with a most exemplary patience. The Republican party does claim, and has always claimed, and the Democratic party always claimed until about the year 1852, throughout all the North, that Congress had plenary and unquestionable power, under the Constitution of the United States, to prohibit negro slavery in Territories, and that it is the duty of Congress to exert that power whenever slavery did not exist in any Territory where the white man could live and work. My Democratic friend from Ohio [Mr. VALLANDIGHAM] stated here, a few days ago, that the Democratic party had been wrong upon that subject—meaning that they had heretofore conceded this power, and insisted on its exercise. Now, it is certain, to look at it historically, that, in the progress of your Government, the first founders of it did proceed upon that principle. The ordinance of 1787 was made under the old Confederation; it was made by very many of the men who sat in the Convention which formed the present Constitution of the United States; and Virginia, by all her delegates, voted for that ordinance.

Mr. MILLSON. There is no doubt, as the gentleman from Ohio [Mr. CORWIN] has remarked, that the opinions which he has imputed to Washington, Jefferson, and other distinguished statesmen of the ante-revolutionary period, were entertained by them. But it should be remembered that it was before the abolition of the African slave trade that those views were expressed. It was while standing in the living presence of the victims of that traffic that their opinions were formed. It was natural, sir, and almost unavoidable, that they should think on slavery only as a part of that legalized system of rapine and plunder. They at least would regard it as the motive prompting men to the perpetration of crime. They did not see slavery as we see it. Indeed, sir, it was not then, as it is now, a social system established between two classes of our own native population, intended to promote the welfare and happiness of both; an institution of society, establishing a just and wise subordination and dependence between two races, living together in almost equal numbers, who socially never could be equal, and whom, therefore, political equality would convert into fierce and implacable enemies.

Mr. CORWIN. I thank the gentleman. That is what I was going to say myself, but the gentleman has expressed it much better than I should have done it. I was about to refer to that ordinance of 1787, whence I deduce the conclusion that the men of that day did believe that it was the best thing they could do with the five States provided for in that ordinance, to prohibit negro slavery there.

Mr. SMITH, of Virginia. Will the gentleman permit me to say a word here? Mr. Madison expressly states that the object of that prohibition was to take away the field left open for the importation of Africans.

Mr. CORWIN. I was about to speak of that opinion of Mr. Madison. I know from conversations, which even so young a man as myself has had with the men of that period, that Virginia had some reasons for agreeing to the prohibition of slavery in that part of the Territory, altogether unconnected with the institution of slavery. But I shall insist that the main reasons were the objection to slavery itself. Virginia was then a great State, as she is now. "There were giants in those days." She was afraid that the rich lands of the Northwest, with slavery tolerated there, would induce eminent men whom she had at home, to go there; and she did not wish to part with those illustrious men. She wished to keep them where they were. Virginia wanted then, as she wants now, and as every State wants, to keep as much greatness and as much glory in their old homes as possible. Something like that was in operation then. But I can hardly suppose that that was the controlling motive with the great men who did that great act. Their often-expressed abhorrence of slavery proves it was not. A great act it was for good, for lasting good, as subsequent events have shown. It was provided that all the States that were to come into the Federal Union under that ordinance should prohibit slavery; and it was under that provision that Ohio, the first State that came in under it, excluded slavery in her State Constitution.

Now, what did the men of that day believe? They were wise men, philosophic statesmen. The terrific storm of the Revolution had blown over them; and we all know that the minds of men, after having been much agitated, and relieved from the causes of that agitation, then become so calm that in no period of their lives are they so well situated for cool reason or calm reflection as immediately after such an event. They were Americans. They were Republicans; I do not use the terms in a party sense. They called themselves Republicans. We call ourselves so now; and we do believe we are following in our principles this day right after them. What I beg anybody to convince me of is, that I am mistaken. When so convinced, if that be possible, I shall surely acknowledge my mistake, and abandon my present convictions. The great, the good as well as great men of 1787 ordained by law that there never should be any slavery in that part of Virginia which had been ceded to the United States by the deed of 1784. Would they have done so, if they had considered slavery to be a good institution? I think not. There was no overruling necessity for such a prohibition, arising out of circumstances unconnected with slavery. It was their belief that the greatest blessing they could bestow upon these five new States was the prohibition of negro slavery. They thought that an industrious, intelligent community of free white men, having no degraded labor among them, was the best community that could be established. I suppose they had read Montesquieu, and believed with him that without virtue, honesty, and intelligence, a Republic is impossible. I suppose that is a maxim on which everybody agrees. They believed that sort of system would be best promoted in a country where white men can work, by saying that there should be no forced labor there.

I am not considering *now* whether or not these great men were mistaken. I only wish, at this point, to say, that this much-abused Republican party, so much misunderstood to-day, is acting exactly as these men acted in 1787, who, whether under the Constitution or under the Articles of Confederation, forbade slavery in all the Northwestern country, and forbade it because they thought it, as all their declarations at that time prove, a great evil. I mean to say—and I hope all sides of this House will understand me to say—is, that if the men of 1787 had believed that slavery was not only a benign institution, but one that was friendly to the white man in that climate, they would not have prohibited it. They were not the kind of men to do anything for party expediency. They were not contending as to who should hammer this House to order. They were laying deep the foundations of this mighty Empire; and they acted under the profound responsibility which such a condition of things imposed. They spoke with sincerity, they acted with sincerity, in the presence of that God who they believed, and I believe, had most manifestly bared his right arm in every battle-field of the Revolution in favor of our right of self-government and independence. They, then, seeing that there was a territory not yet comprehended within the limits of any State, having no power to do anything as a State, prohibited the existence of slavery therein. That is what they did; and such men must have done that act for the reason that they believed it right, and thought, as we Republicans think, that slavery is a great evil, at least in any climate where white men and free laborers *can* live and work.

That territory of Virginia, which she claimed under a very old charter, was no longer the territory of Virginia. It was regarded as territory acquired by the common blood and treasure of the people of the Confederacy, just as your territories won from Mexico; and, under these circumstances, they then declared: "We will, under this Confederation, agree that there shall be no slavery in this territory, thus won by the common blood and treasure of us all." They so ordained; and they made it a matter of compact forever between the existing Government and the States to be formed out of that territory, that every such State should always exclude slavery. I do not say what effect that would have under our modern notions about compacts. Perhaps, in modern times, we might believe that a State, after it came into the Union, no matter what bargain it made to get in, was such a mysterious and omnipotent sovereign, that all obligations passed from it, and ceased to have binding effect. Be this as it may, my purpose is now to show what were the views of those men, the founders of our Government, respecting slavery. That is the fact I wish to show.

Now, then, suppose another Territory to be acquired by the common blood and the common treasure of the United States, in a latitude like that of the Northwestern Territory. The Republican party say, "We will exclude slavery from that Territory, as the framers of the Constitution under the Confederation did exclude it from just such territory as that." And if we do that, are we to be charged with an attempt wilfully to subvert the institutions of this country and to do wrong to the South? If those Old Fathers of the Revolution—our Fathers, the Fathers of our nation, the authors of all that we boast of, and all that is around us—if they acted in this way, may you not pardon us for doing just as they did? Are we not, at least, excusable for entertaining the opinion that it would be better to confine the institution to its present limits, or certainly to exclude it from a new Territory, as they did? If you think they acted well and wisely upon this subject, it is your duty, under like circumstances, to imitate their example, not calculating too curiously, as they did not, about a few dollars' worth of slave property, which you may not be able to sell to, or carry with you into each Territory; but considering, as they did, and pondering, deeply and profoundly, what is to be the effect upon the people who are to live in the Territories, from generation to generation and from time to time, during the whole period of man's history in the world. Well, you will say, they may have been wrong. Admit that irreverent, preposterous supposition, and answer me, boastful, self-sufficient Democracy, do you blame us for having an affectionate regard for the memory of those old men, and a fixed belief that their acts were wisely and well done, and might be safely imitated by the Democratic sages of 1860? I hope you will not say that I am out of order, on either side of the House, when I declare, in the presence of God, that I do believe, that if we had twenty of these very men in this House, this question would not even be mooted, and we should have organized in one day. We do not work as they worked, we do not talk like them; and, worst of all, we do not think as they thought.

Why are we, I ask again, to be denounced as bad men for desiring to act as our fathers acted? We wish to do just what they did under similar circumstances. We desire, if the country give us the power, to do all things rightly; and in doing so, we turn to the bright examples of better days for our guide. Unhappily for us, the North and the South have no confidence in each other, and madness rules the hour. You think you have diverse and opposing interests. This is all a mistake—a great mistake. Whatever promotes the interest of Alabama and Mississippi is, in a national point of view, equally favorable to the interest of the State of Ohio. One gentleman has spoken of Ohio as an Empire State. If she be such a State, is not Alabama made stronger by her connection with a strong rather than a weak State? In any national conflict, Alabama has a powerful ally. In this view, it is too plain for argument that every State is interested in the prosperity of every other, and each in the prosperity and happiness of all. We are not rivals, we are brothers. And here, I may ask, without egotism, why is young Ohio so powerful? Kentucky is older by many years; whilst, with a climate and soil unsurpassed by few, perhaps none, in the Union; with a people surpassed by no community for enterprise, for courage, for constancy, for all the qualities which give character and influence and just pride to States, Ohio certainly, from some cause, has very far exceeded her elder sister in developing wealth, population, and all that constitutes a strong and powerful State. Why is this so? The cause, I think, will be found in facts which give Ohio no cause to boast of herself, but in that very institution which forms the topic of all this debate. Kentucky is my native State. I knew her well; I knew her great men, and love them and honor them; but Ohio and her, side by side, joined in heart as well as neighborhood—look at them, and you will see the difference between them to which I refer. There is history, that may be studied with profit, touching this matter.

My colleague [Mr. Cox] spoke of a meeting upon the western reserve in Ohio. He is a young gentleman, a rising man, and, if he does not get bad habits upon the Democratic side of the House, may come to something some day hence. [Laughter.] He amused himself with the comic power he possesses in imitating the nasal twang of the Yankees of that reserve. It sounded strange to you, as it did to him, and so it did to the army of Prince Rupert at Marston Moor, when the ancestors of these men rushed into battle against the mailed chivalry and curled darlings of the court of Charles I. What happened then? Something worthy to be noted, and not forgotten. Stout Cromwell and his unconquerable Ironsides, when the day was well nigh lost, charged with resistless fury upon the proud columns of that host of gentlemen, as they were boastfully denominated, and lo! Prince Rupert and his host were no longer there. They were scattered as the dried leaves of autumn are before the storm-blast of the coming winter. That same nasal twang rang out, on that day, their well-known war cry, "the sword of the Lord and Gideon." These Yankees are a peculiar people; they are an industrious, thriving, pains-taking race of men. The frailties of these men grow out of their very virtues, those stern virtues which founded liberty in England, and baptized it in their own blood upon Bunker Hill, in America. They will do so again, if there is a necessity for it. It is a hard matter to deal with men who do verily believe that God Almighty and his Angels encamp round about them. What do they care for earthly things or earthly power? What do they care for Kings, and Lords, and Presidents? They fully believe they are heirs of the King of Kings. In the hour of battle, they seem to themselves to stand, like the great Hebrew leader, in the cleft of the rock; the glory of the most high God passes by them, and they catch a gleam of its brightness. If you come in conflict with the purposes of such men, they will regard duty as everything, life as nothing. So it appeared in our war of the Revolution.

The gentleman from Mississippi [Mr. Barksdale] says that the North got more Revolutionary pensions than the South. I do not know how that is. How did it happen? Gentlemen tell me they would not have pensions in the South. I am glad if it be so. I happen to know professionally something of revolutionary claims for lands. Virginia, when she ceded the Northwestern Territory to the United States, reserved all the lands lying between the Little Miami and Scioto rivers, to satisfy the claims of her troops in the Virginia line on continental establishment. A large district in Kentucky had been taken up to satisfy the same class of claims. All the reservation in Ohio has been absorbed, and still land warrants come, and scrip has been granted; and yet the Virginia line on continental establishment is not yet satisfied. Sir, it has seemed to us that the army of Xerxes might have all claimed and been satisfied before this time. But this is all aside and apart from the proper subject before us. I am not now, never have been, and never will be, one to so far violate history and good taste as to draw invidious distinctions between this or that State or colony, who, by their combined valor, won the independence of all the States. While I must always venerate the men of New England of that day, I still turn with unabated admiration to those of the South, especially to Virginia—glorious "Old Dominion," illustrious alike for her heroes in war and her sages in peace; and if it depend on vote or effort of mine, the last land warrant of the last descendant of her revolutionary heroes shall be located on lands, if such can be found, rich as the delta of the Nile; in a climate, if it be possible, healthful as was Eden ere yet sin had brought death into the home of the first family of man.

Mr. Clerk, it is my wish to show that the Republican party, which proposes to prohibit slavery in *Territories*, is in that principle following the example of the men of the Revolutionary period, both before and after the adoption of the Constitution. The ordinance of 1787, prior to, or rather cotemporary with, the Constitution, shows that the men who, under the Confederation, enacted that ordinance, thought it most wise and beneficial towards slave and free States both, to prohibit slavery in the Northwestern Territory. Now, if those men were wise men—if they were patriots—then what is the Republican party? It proposes to continue their *policy;* to imitate their example; to follow in their footsteps; and this is all on the subject of slavery which we propose to do. Were the men of 1787 wrong, then indeed in this particular is the Republican party wrong. If they were right in the *policy* which dictated the ordinance of 1787, then is the Republican party right, and the Democratic party wrong—totally, entirely wrong. But you say this ordinance was not enacted under the Constitution, but prior to it; and that, under and by virtue of the Constitution, we have no power to prohibit slavery in Territories by acts of Congress. Let us now see what the fathers *said* on that subject; and, particularly, let us observe what they *did*. I must insist on the point of examining into what the elder men of the Republic did, for this reason: those men made, pondered, studied, adopted, the Constitution. They had great veneration for it; and all of them who acted under it, whether in legislative, executive, or judicial capacity, took a solemn oath to *support* and not to *violate* it. If they were honest, (and I think that we will scarcely dispute it,) then, if they did violate the Constitution, they were *ignorant* men, and did not understand their own work as well as we *sages* here assembled. I think the characteristic modesty of this House will scarcely assert the latter proposition!

Passing by many facts in our political history which threw some light on the subject before, let us pause a moment at the year 1820. Not long before this time, we had passed through our second war with Great Britain. At that time, I began to look out upon the political affairs of the world with that interest which both novelty and importance would inspire in all young minds. I read the arguments in the Missouri case with a great deal of care. Although the sentiment of the country was generally against me, I then formed the opinion that Missouri had a *right* to come into the Union with slavery. I thought that right was founded upon the treaty stipulations by which that Territory was acquired. The treaty, ratified as it was by the Senate, two-thirds of that body concurring, became, in the language of the Constitution, the "supreme law of the land." What was Louisiana when we acquired her? Anybody, who knows the history of the times, will know what she was. A little settlement, old, it is true, but so small in population that it would be made by the Yankees of this day in a very few months. What was the reason of that acquisition? All who have looked into the current history of the West, from 1790 up to about 1803, know that Western men, the ancestors of those who now boast so much of our loyalty to the Union, were threatening to break off from those now living east of the Alleghanies, and to make an independent confederation west of it, and to force free trade to the sea through the mouth of the Mississippi. Jefferson was alarmed, and the whole country was alarmed, as you will see if you read the debates of 1802 and 1803, in and out of Congress, while this matter was going on. Everybody West demanded that we should go into war with Spain, because she would not let us trade through the mouth of the Mississippi; and most eloquent and impressive speeches were made, enforcing the idea that there was danger of a Western secession, unless trade was made easy to the Gulf of Mexico through the Mississippi river. Mr. Jefferson, without any constitutional authority whatever, as he himself thought and openly avowed, authorized our Ministers in France to negotiate for the purchase of Louisiana, which had then but recently fallen into the hands of France. It was to avoid war that it was done. That was the motive. It seems, by the subsequent purchases of Flordia, and more recently of California and New Mexico, that there was authority for acquisition all the while lurking in the treaty-making and war-making powers.

I doubt very much, Mr. Clerk, whether the First Consul, that Little Corporal who was in command in France at that time, would have ever signed a treaty which abrogated any right that the people of the ceded territory then had. We know that when the treaty was completed, it has been always said, and I believe it, that Napoleon refused to put his signature to it, unless we agreed to admit the people of Louisiana into our confederacy of States, with all the rights enjoyed by those who were already in the Union. He was in arms for liberty then; he proclaimed himself then "the armed soldier of freedom," and would not have given up that colony, as he called it, for all you could have offered him, but that he had no navy to protect it. He was at war with England, and he knew that England with her navy would take his colonies from him. He was therefore glad to get rid of them. That Territory would have been a point of weakness to France then, just as Canada would be a point of weakness to England now, if she were in a war with us. That was Napoleon's idea, and that article in the treaty which secured to Louisiana the right to enter into the Confederacy, was inserted at the request of Napoleon, and, no doubt, at that time, it showed his sincere admiration of our Government. He would not sign the treaty till that was put in, in such terms as (treaties being the supreme law of the land) must prevail over any of our notions of slavery. And Louisiana and Missouri would not have been admitted at that day without that clause in the treaty, although I think, without such treaty, they would in time have been admitted without it. I do not say that it was the policy or the wish of the founders of the Republic to disturb the relations of property that existed when they acquired any territory. They left Louisiana just as it was; so they did with Florida, in 1819. Slaves were property there when we acquired that territory and they remained property; and Florida came into the Union with slavery. Arkansas was admitted in the same way. But in that part of the country comprehended within the Louisiana purchase lying north of latitude 36° 30′, covered by what is called the Missouri compromise line there was no population—no white men, no slaves no property to be affected; and therefore slavery could properly be prohibited there. That was the view which the men of 1820 took of that subject. That has been called a compromise and the legislation of 1850 has been called a *compromise.* Why, I know not. I apprehend that none of the men of that day voted for a law which they believed compromised away or violated the Constitution of the United States Certainly, no Congress should be lightly charged with such horrible infidelity to themselves and their posterity. They never thought they were violating the Constitution, and compromising it when they passed the Missouri restriction. They maintained their position of justice and fidelity to compacts. The Constitution had declared that that Constitution, and the treaties and laws made under it, should be the supreme law of the land overruling all other laws. That omnipotent treaty-making power was not trusted to anything short of two-thirds of that great constitutional body, the Senate of the United States. It was safe to trust it to two-thirds of that body, representing all the sovereign States of the Union.

I have attempted to explain, Mr. Clerk, that we acquired territory, that slavery existed in it as an institution, and that there never was any exercise of the powers of the Government to destroy that local institution, or, if you please, that right The whole of the Louisiana purchase, so far as slavery was concerned, was left just as it was acquired until 1821, when slavery was prohibited north of 36° 30′. Whether any slaves were held in the country to which the inhibition applied, it is not material, at this day, to decide. My impression is, there were none. However, the men of 1820–'21 understood all about the early settlements in the "Louisiana purchase," and the character of those settlements also, much better than we can be supposed to understand them after a lapse of forty years. We know that the men of that day declared that the treaty by which we acquired that territory contained provisions by which we were bound, its obligations being paramount to all law and every other obligation They admitted Missouri, as I think she would have been admitted if there had been no treaty; perhaps it might not have been within a year or two, but eventually I believe she would have been admitted without the aid of treaty stipulations.

Now, sir, who were *they*, disputing at that time about this question of the benefits of slavery, the disadvantages of slavery, the evils of slavery, looking at it in all its aspects, social, moral political? They were the men of 1820; they were men who had just emerged from that struggle with Great Britain, second in importance, as they thought, only to that in which they conquered our independence; they rejoiced that they had come out of it with reputation to the country. Their hearts were American. Whether Democrats, Republicans, or Federalists, they were all Americans; all party lines had been obliterated. We know that the period to which I refer was called the halcyon period of the Republic. God knows it *was* a happy day in the public affairs, compared with the present. What did they do? Just what we should do to-morrow, if we were like them. They admitted a slave State because they were bound to do it, either by treaty obligations or by those fraternal relations that must exist between the States; and they said that slavery should never exist in the territory north of Missouri.

You of the South insist that the inhibition of slavery in the territory north of the State of Missouri was unconstitutional. Is it to be supposed that the men of those days did not understand their constitutional obligations? There were Mr. Monroe, and John Quincy Adams, and William H. Crawford—my Georgia friends can understand who I mean when I speak of him—a man, in my memory, quite as illustrious as any citizen that has ever lived in that great State. He was Secretary of the Treasury in the Cabinet of Mr. Monroe. There was Mr. Smith Thompson, afterwards Judge of the Supreme Court—a man whom everybody who knew him will now remember as one possessing great learning in matters of constitutional law, as well as in the common and civil law; a jurist, in the best sense of the word; an old-fashioned man, in the best sense of the word; a man of large and well-furnished head, and sound, patriotic heart. He was Secretary of the Navy. Mr. McLean was not at that time a member of the Cabinet. It remained for Gen. Jackson to bring the Postmaster General into the Cabinet, but he was in familiar association with that Cabinet. But who was he, I ask you, whose only function it was, at that time, to give constitutional law to the Cabinet? Who was the Attorney General, who has nothing else to do but that, or would have nothing else to do, if we had not imposed extra-official duties upon him? William Wirt was the man, a Virginian. I presume my honorable friend from Virginia, who sits before me now, [Mr. Bocock,] would have had some doubt about the propriety of his own opinion upon legal and constitutional points, if Mr. Wirt had differed from him.

John C. Calhoun, of South Carolina, was also a member of that Cabinet. This very question, the power of Congress to prohibit slavery in the Territories, was submitted to that Cabinet. Was Mr. Monroe an Abolitionist? Doubtless, like others of his compeers of that period, he did entertain the opinion, that wherever the white man could labor with advantage, it would be better to prohibit slavery; but that was not the question submitted to him—him of the revolutionary era; him, an honored and influential patriot, from the time of our independence up to the constitutional era; him, a cotemporary of the Constitution itself, who knew all the motives and reasons, the *pros* and *cons*, why this power was put in, and that was left out, of that instrument—which, as was eloquently remarked the other day, is so delicate a piece of machinery, that, if it be deranged in a single spring, the whole falls into chaos. This man, a cotemporary of that period, who had studied that complex and delicate work, knew the object of the whole and the function of each of its parts—I ask, did he not understand the uses and design of that work as well, nay, much better, than we, his degenerate successors? That question, I repeat, was submitted to his Cabinet, not a single member of which, I believe, is now alive; and the testimony of Mr. Adams is, that they were unanimously of the opinion that the bill prohibiting slavery in the territory north of latitude 36° 30′ was a constitutional law.

Mr. KEITT, (in his seat.) Mr. Calhoun denied the statement.

Mr. CORWIN. I heard the gentleman from South Carolina make that statement the other day. I was in the Senate when that was mentioned. If my memory be correct, Mr. Calhoun said, at that time, he did not remember that fact. But be that as it may, if Mr. Calhoun at that time had entertained the opinion that it was not within the constitutional competency of Congress to pass that act, is it likely, from the earnest nature and character of the man, that he would not have left on record his protest against the approval of what he might have deemed an unconstitutional law?

Mr. KEITT. I will quote a single word from Mr. Monroe's testimony. It is not quite so strong as I thought it was, but it is just it should be quoted. It is:

"That the proposed restriction of Territories 'which are to be admitted into the Union, if 'not in direct violation of the Constitution, is 'repugnant to its principles."

Mr. CORWIN. I have not brought myself to the conclusion that Mr. Monroe put his name to a bill that he believed unconstitutional.

From the history of the times to which I now refer, we should all learn to tolerate difference of opinion. Mr. Jefferson thought a great public necessity obliged him to acquire Louisiana, without any warrant in the Constitution for that act. It is not necessary now to recur to the historical facts of that day which formed in the mind of Mr. Jefferson a justification of that act. Louisiana was thus acquired, and all then supposed our territory complete. But after the war of 1812 was ended, we found, or thought we found, another necessity. Florida was a Spanish colony. She was our neighbor, our too near neighbor. Our race, our rapacious race, will not submit to a close proximity with any other race. Many apologies and some reasons were soon found why we should own Florida. Indians abounded there; slaves were *property* there. It was said, and I believe with truth, that these Indians would sometimes steal or spirit away the slaves of our adjoining States, or that slaves would run away into Florida, and fugitive slave bills, as we knew, could not be enforced there. Florida was purchased to adjust this difficulty. Slavery was lawful there, and the Government received it, kept it, and to this day does not pretend to disturb slavery in Florida. It may be remembered that the legislative power of Congress over Territories came before the Supreme Court of the United States as a question directly or incidentally involved in a case which was brought from that Territory, I think in the year 1828. The whole court then agreed that Congress alone could legislate for Territories. It should be borne in mind that this was the same court, but not the same judges, which decided the famous case of Dred Scott. What did Mexico say when she ceded territory to us? She ceded it to the United States; not to South Carolina, or to Georgia, or Massachusetts; but to the United States. She said that the right to make laws for this people is now transferred to the United States. The local laws and regulations in all such cases remain in full force, except where they conflict with the Constitution of the United States. The deed of cession was made to the *Government of the United States*, and that Government, by consequence, has, by virtue of treaty, the power to control the territory. I have given you the opinion of Chief Justice Marshall. There are other decisions of the Supreme Court, which I may hereafter refer to, recognising Congress as the only legislative power which can rightfully make laws for a Territory, until that *Territory* becomes a *State*.

Now, let me look a little to our opinions—the opinions of learned gentlemen elected to represent the people. It was observed by the gentleman from Mississippi, that, in the "compromise" of 1850, as he will continue to call it, the power to make laws for the Territories was abandoned. Now, if any one will look into the laws of 1850, organizing the Territories of New Mexico and Utah, they will find that, while they organized a Legislative Council and a lower House of Representatives, in each of those organic laws they provide, "*that the laws made by the Territorial Legislature should be returned to Congress, and if disapproved by Congress, should be null and void.*" So far from surrendering this great principle, now become established by judicial decision as well as by the laws of Congress, Congress expressly retained the power to annul the laws of the Territory. Sir, I listened to the debates upon those measures of 1850 for many months. Mr. Webster was, I think, very unjustly condemned by a portion of the people of his own State, because, they said, he surrendered this great right. I have lived too long to be much amazed at anything; but I have been utterly astonished that it should have been asserted by any one that either of the illustrious men who figured in that discussion—Clay or Webster—ever surrendered the *power* of Congress to prohibit slavery in the Territories of the United States. They declared, in their speeches, that they believed they had that power; but that the territory coming from Mexico was free, and that no power on earth, except Congress, could take slavery there, unless the law-making power of that territory had planted it there before we acquired it. All the courts, State and Federal, up to 1854, had determined that slavery is the creature of local law, or long local usage recognised as lawful, which was but another formula for the expression of that principle.

[At this point, Mr. CORWIN gave way for a motion to adjourn.]

Tuesday, January 24, 1860.

Mr. CLERK: I ought to apologize to the House and to myself for suffering myself to be beguiled into this debate without any preparation whatever. I ought not to have been drawn into this discussion without some preparation. When Sir Walter Scott was inquired of, why he did not write the Life of Napoleon in one volume, instead of three, he replied, that he had not the time. If I had known that I should have been brought to discuss the very questions that have been in my mind since I took the floor yesterday, or that I should have said anything to the House, except merely call its attention to the necessity of electing a Speaker, I certainly would have said in one hour what required two hours to accomplish yesterday. I wish now, before I proceed, having collected myself somewhat during the intervening time since the adjournment, to ask the gentleman from Virginia, [Mr. GARNETT,] whether I understood him yesterday to say that Mr. Jefferson, at some time in his life, had expressed the opinion that the Missouri restriction was unconstitutional, or only that it was inexpedient.

Mr. GARNETT. Both.

Mr. CORWIN. When I conceded that such was his opinion, I did not mean to say that Mr. Jefferson had said at any time that the law passed, restricting slavery beyond a certain line of latitude, was unconstitutional. I did know that he had somewhere expressed the opinion that it was highly inexpedient. If such an opinion as that suggested by the gentleman from Virginia was ever expressed by Mr. Jefferson, I do not know it. That he declared the acquisition of the Territory of Louisiana to be without warrant of Constitution, is a matter of such public political history that none of us are ignorant of it. But I do not mean to concede the point that Mr. Jefferson had expressly declared the Missouri act unconstitutional.

Now, Mr. Clerk, let us recall what I intended to present to the world—for we always speak to mankind when we speak in Congress, and to all posterity, and to all time back of us, if it can be made to hear. I have endeavored to apologize to my friends upon the other side of the House for the very erroneous opinions, as they call them, of the so-called Republican party. I only want to say to them now, that we must be excused if we take the same ground with the fathers of the Revolution and the fathers of the Constitution; and that whatever may be the opinions of the men on that side of the House, we cannot find it in our consciences to accuse ourselves of treason while we advocate the doctrines of Washington, of Jefferson, of Madison, and of Monroe. We may be wrong upon the point of law; we may be wrong about the power of Congress; but about the *policy* of restricting slavery, we being wrong, those great men were wrong. If they were right, beyond peradventure the Democratic party are wrong. That was the view which I wished to present to my fellow-citizens assembled here—to my fellow-members—by way of excusing us from listening hereafter to charges of treason, murder, robbery, and arson, which have been charged upon the whole Republican party. Why, the arguments of some of these gentlemen on the other side would indicate that, in their opinion, as a matter of criminal law, every one of the Republicans could be convicted of being at Harper's Ferry, with a pike in his hand, pushing it into the bosom of a Southern gentleman. [Laughter.] Sir, it made me feel a little unhappy at first, until I found that all this was said in joke; yet the world, which is listening to this debate, do not understand this. Gentlemen tell us here that they mean nothing personal by these remarks. "It is true," say these gentlemen, "that you do commit treason, you 'do commit arson, murder, and all these crimes, 'but you do it in the most honorable and honest 'way." [Laughter.] That is satisfactory to me.

Sir, I endeavored to show yesterday, by reference to the general history of the country, that Mr. SEWARD had said nothing, that Helper had said nothing, more offensive than Washington. I do not know what is in Helper's book, except by report. I was written to by one of my constituents for a copy of that new book, about which he had heard so much. I had been listening to this argument about treason, and I said to my constituent that I had no copy, except one, and that it would be dangerous for it to go through the post office with my frank. I should be afraid that it would be brought up as testimony against me, under an indictment by some court in Virginia, for being an accessory after the fact, by sending Helper's book under my frank to Green county, Ohio. And that is not all. There would be the evidence that I nominated my colleague, [Mr. SHERMAN,] and voted for him. I hope gentlemen will see the delicacy of my situation. I have much feeling on this subject. I have a wife and children, and they do not want me hung for voting for my worthy colleague. [Laughter.] It would not be agreeable to them. [Renewed laughter.]

I think I had shown yesterday, by the references which I made, that nothing has been said by Mr. SEWARD which could be construed as offensive to the South as these declarations of Jefferson, which are known by heart throughout the length and breadth of the entire Union. Now, I wish to address to gentlemen on the other side of the House one or two suggestions upon a question of logic and fair reason. They say that Mr. SEWARD, being the head and leader of the Republican party—against my protestations, they constantly deny me that honor, [laughter]—had proclaimed at Rochester, in general terms, that between forced labor and free labor there necessarily would be some collision; that some conflict would go on between them; and that, in consequence of that doctrine, John Brown determined to murder somebody at Harper's Ferry. Now, do they suppose that John Brown had not read Jefferson's Notes on Virginia, and all other things which Jefferson had written about slavery? Do they suppose he had not seen the declaration of Washington, that if there were any way by which slavery could be abolished, he would render to it his cordial co-operation? Do you suppose he had not seen that? Do you suppose he had not seen the debates in the Convention, in which slavery is denounced as an enormous evil leading step by step, as certainly and as steadily as the step of time, to a consummation as fatal as death? Do you suppose John Brown had not read all these things in his solitude among the mountains of New York, where, twenty years ago, he says, he first conceived the idea of invading one of the Southern States, and carrying off its slaves? Do you suppose he had not pondered upon these things, and prayed over them—for he was a praying man, as all enthusiasts are? He was a brave man, as all stern enthusiasts are; and it was because he thought this enterprise, the offspring of his gloomy imagination, was consecrated by the approbation of Jefferson and Washington, that, as he sometimes said, be believed the arms of the Almighty upheld him, he was encompassed about by the Angels of the Lord.

Is all this to be attributed to a declaration of Mr. SEWARD, in reference to a conflict between slave and free labor? I appeal to gentlemen, if they could trace back Brown's conduct at Harper's Ferry to any source out of his own solitary meditations, whatever others might have stated of their opinions, whether it is not more rational to trace the germ of that conduct to those writings, speeches, and letters, of your own great men of the South? They were great men; they were heroes. They were the great men of the United States, and the great men of the world; and, notwithstanding you have changed your opinion on the subject of slavery, and made it contrary to theirs, yet their names, and their fame, and their opinions, will be engraved upon the pages of history when those of us of this date shall be buried in profound oblivion. [Applause upon the floor and in the galleries.] It is wonderful that the talent, ingenuity, and eloquence, of this discussion should have come to such conclusions. Shall our minds be fastened upon these flimsy pretences, when we know there was matter enough in the writings and speeches of the foremost men of the world to stimulate a mind like John Brown's into frantic fanaticism?

But it is said we are accessories after the fact. I ask gentlemen if they have not attached too much importance to the Helper book? When Thomas Paine was indicted in England, Attorney General McDonald, I believe, well known in forensic history, gave him some notice of the fact that he was to be tried for a libel upon the British Government in the publication of his pamphlet, "The Rights of Man." A friend of Paine advised him to go over immediately and make some compromise with the Government. "No," said he, "that indictment is an advertisement, and one hundred thousand copies of that pamphlet will be in circulation in three weeks." And so it happened. Those one hundred thousand copies would not have seen the light, if it had not been for the indiscreet conduct of the then Attorney General of the British Cabinet. So such matters work out; and so it must ever be in a country where principles are free, and speech and press are free. While on this subject, let me say what, I think, will be agreed to by every considerate man in the House and out of it. Suppose all of the two hundred and thirty-seven gentlemen here had met upon some concern of great interest to us personally. Suppose that some man was proposed to discharge a certain duty for us, and it was known that this gentleman had said or done something which might possibly be an objection to him for the discharge of the duty to be assigned to him. Any man who was a friend of his would have taken him aside, (as the gentleman from Missouri might have done,) and said: "Now, Mr. SHERMAN, you have been nominated by a highly-respectable gentleman from Ohio." [Laughter.] That is what I would have said. Then he would have gone on: "I should have no doubts about voting for you; 'but I understand you have recommended a book 'which teaches insurrection and rebellion in the 'slave States. How did you come to do it?" Mr. SHERMAN would have taken that gentleman by the hand, and said: "Sir, a gentleman on this floor 'from New York came to me, while I was hastily doing some business at my desk, and told 'me it was desirable to collate certain parts of a 'book called 'Helper's Impending Crisis,' and 'to publish them in a cheap pamphlet, which 'pamphlet was to have a political effect"—that is, to illustrate, I suppose, the doctrines of the Republican party. I suppose that is what they all understood. "I asked him," Mr. SHERMAN would say, "is it all proper, all right? Said my 'friend, 'certainly.' Then, without looking at 'the book, and knowing nothing about it, I authorized him to put my name to a recommendation of a book yet to be written. When I saw 'the work, I did not endorse it. I am sorry that 'I was thoughtlessly and unwittingly brought 'into this recommendation of it. I never intended to endorse such a book. The gentleman from New York told me it was all right."

Sir, I do think, under that explanation, the gentleman from Missouri would have taken his seat, and said, "After all stated in the New 'York *Herald*, there is nothing against Mr. SHERMAN, except that he acted unadvisedly, for which 'he is now sorry." He would not, if he had been his political friend, have risen and menaced him with a criminal prosecution. Criminal conduct is always to be found in the intention of men. I subscribe to a newspaper, to be printed for six months or a year; I put my name to the subscription, and recommend it. It turns out that the editor is a rascal and a blackguard. Am I to be held responsible for what is published in that paper? I think the *argumentum ad hominem* might put some gentlemen on the other side in a very odd position. The gentleman from Ohio recommended the publication of a book—not a book which had been printed, but a book to be made out of another, which he never saw in his life until this resolution of the gentleman from Missouri was offered. Well, gentlemen say there is nothing to stain Mr. SHERMAN'S honor; and yet, honored as he is, and unstained as he is in that particular respect, if he should be elected as Speaker of this House, it would be a burning shame; the Union might be dissolved, and civil war take place.

Mr. McCLERNAND. Who said that?

Mr. CLARK, of Missouri. I ask the gentleman this question: Do you assert that I ever said so?

Mr. CORWIN. I was arguing upon the general tenor of the speeches on the other side of the House.

Mr. CLARK, of Missouri. I understood the gentlemen to say that I so asserted.

Mr. CORWIN. No, sir; not at all. I do not think anybody stated that, in terms.

Mr. CLARK, of Missouri. Has anybody upon this floor said so?

Mr. CORWIN. No, sir. I said you argued that civil war must come thus: the election of Mr. SHERMAN—that was the first step; the next will be the election of Mr. SEWARD; and then, war.

Mr. CLARK, of Missouri. The gentleman never heard me assert that.

Mr. CORWIN. No, sir; it was said by other gentlemen on that side. You may not have heard it.

Mr. KEITT, (in his seat.) Plenty of them, often and again.

Mr. CORWIN. I do not certainly misrepresent gentlemen in what I have said. Now, what is to follow? We, the Republican party, if we can, shall certainly elect these men, or somebody just like them. I wish to know what the *casus belli* is to be, before we set out; but all you can say, all the world can say, will never prevent any freeman in any free State—or slave State, I hope, either—from exercising the right of suffrage just when and as he pleases. No menace from any man, or a number of men living at my own door in Ohio, I trust, will ever avail to induce me to surrender that great inalienable right, or shrink with a craven timidity from its free exercise. I can assure those who threaten disunion, because the North or the West shall chance to vote for whom they deem proper for President, that no more fatal mistake ever entered into the head of a maniac, than the supposition that *threats* from any or all other quarters of the United States will prevent or deter a freemen in the North or West from voting according to the dictate of his own unbiassed sense of duty to himself and his country.

Mr. Clerk, yesterday I intended to bring before the House the constitutional doctrines held by the Republican party, and compare them with the doctrines held by the founders of the Republic, and thus endeavor to prove, that when we declare that Congress, under our Constitution, has the power to prohibit slavery in the *Territories* of the United States, before they become States, we propose nothing which is new, either in the principles or policy of those who founded this Government; and that the practice and policy of this Government, up to the year 1854, is in accordance with the doctrines now held by the Republican party of this day. I am sure that the history of the Government, in all its departments—legislative, judicial, and executive—will sustain me in this position. If so, then I shall feel authorized to inquire of gentlemen on the other side, by what authority you dare to denounce us as holding principles fatal to the peace or interests or liberties of the people? Your apology will be, public opinion is changed; the world has changed its opinions touching slavery. I admit that public opinion may have changed in the South, and public opinion in the North may have been modified somewhat. The public opinion of the world, however, against slavery is stronger now than it was sixty years ago. I know, from the declaration of Mr. Calhoun himself, that his mind did undergo a change in respect to some constitutional points, and in respect to the propriety and morality of the institution of slavery. But do not gentlemen know that ever since the time when Jefferson said, when he contemplated slavery in this country, he "trembled when he remembered that God is just;" that ever since the time when he declared that "nothing was more certainly written in the book of fate, than that the black man one day would be free;" that from that very time, and even before that time, the whole moral sense of the highest minds of England had been running in the very direction of abolitionism? We know, now, that the slave trade never was legalized by any people upon the face of the earth. We learn it from the great debates in the British House of Commons, when the slave trade was prohibited under the auspices of Wilberforce, Granville Sharp, of Pitt, and Fox; we know that the license given by Elizabeth to Hawkins expressly forbid him from bringing a negro from Africa "*by force.*" We know that the statute of George II, which was said to legalize that traffic, forbid that any African should be brought away from Africa except by his own consent. England is not so much to blame as we may suppose for initiating the slave trade, though it is true that she and all Europe acquiesced in it.

Mr. Clerk, we know very well that, in the midst of that universal excitement of the public mind which prevailed during the reign of Elizabeth and subsequent reigns, touching the Protestant and Catholic religions, and the establishment of Protestantism, when all the Powers of Europe were engaged in fighting for the success of the Protestant or Catholic Princes; we know that this affair of the slave trade was a subordinate matter, and passed unnoticed. Had England been in the calm which she enjoyed afterwards in the time of James, I very much doubt whether there ever would have been a negro slave brought from the coast of Africa by force. But it has gone, and England, during the last half of the last century, could not boast of any very great mind in her Parliament who was not opposed to the slave trade. And, as the gentleman from Mississippi well said yesterday, after having abolished the slave trade, the very next step was the abolition of slavery in Jamaica; and I will add, with their views of the subject, they were right. Our crime is, that our notions about slavery, its morality and its evils, are such as these men held. I do not now speak of our right, under the Constitution, to touch it anywhere; that I shall come to by and by. Suppose we do hold opinions touching the evils of slavery in common with the greatest minds that have ever illustrated the history of England—the greatest empire, in my judgment, upon earth—in common with the great minds that founded this Republic. Is it fair, because we have not changed, but still adhere to those old opinions, to charge us with being reptiles, traitors, and serpents? If it is, then dig up from their last resting-place the bones of Jefferson, and hang them up, as royal hatred in England did Cromwell's for many a year. Go to the sacred sarcophagus, now in the hands of the women of this country, and get the bones of Washington to-day, spit upon them, and throw them into the Potomac. He held the opinion that slavery ought to be abolished when it could be done with safety to both master and slave. No Northern man goes further than that. Gentlemen will find that these things will lead us into singular conclusions after a while. I have shown that those opinions were the opinions which illustrate the history of the world, and that they were openly proclaimed by Southern men, too, of whose greatness we all so justly boast.

I endeavored to show yesterday—of which I shall have more to say presently—that Mr. Monroe's administration had sanctioned the very law which the Republican party say shall be passed with reference to the Territories; and that is all they do say. I grant you they stand upon that; that is the only thing which they have ever announced to the world intelligently, and as a matter of law, and doctrine, and practice. It was the departure from that principle which gave birth to the Republican party. I know that in the platform read here the other day by some gentleman on the other side, there was something said about the inalienable rights of man, and there was a long quotation read from the Declaration of Independence. Now, if it has become a crime to quote the Declaration of Independence, pass a law making it so, and we will obey it. I recollect that the celebrated John Randolph once told a young friend of mine, who was traveling with him abroad, that he (this young gentleman) would live to see the day when men would be called to order for quoting the Constitution in Congress.

It seems now, Mr. Clerk, that a gentleman or a party is entirely out of place when he or it quotes the Declaration of Independence with approbation. But I do not construe it as mad enthusiasts do, at all; nor does the Republican party construe it as they do, as paramount to the Constitution. That Declaration says that every man is born with certain inherent, inalienable rights; these are life, liberty, and the pursuit of happiness. I suppose that the Almighty intended man to *live*, or he would not have breathed the breath of life into him. Every man has the right to live, but he certainly may forfeit that right whenever he violates the law. I suppose everybody knows that. I have seen it tried. Man has a right to liberty; but, in my

State of Ohio, if a man breaks a pane of glass, and takes away a piece of goods from a tradesman's store, all that inalienable right, as it is called, cannot save him, and he is sent to serve ten years in the penitentiary, where he never gets the floor, not even for a personal explanation. [Laughter.] Man has a right to the pursuit of happiness, undoubtedly; but if Brigham Young came into the State of Ohio in the pursuit of happiness, in his way, [laughter,] we would lead him off to the penitentiary immediately. All these things are understood by men who analyze them. I know that they are too much abused by men who take occasion to use these general expressions—all of which are true in the sense in which these great men use them. They are truly much abused; but I hope that the Republican party will not be blamed for it, for they have as many men in their ranks who understand them properly as you have. We have schools and colleges in the West; but still we believe that there are men on the eastern slopes of the Atlantic, who, comparatively ignorant though they be, do still comprehend these truths. They have a Bunker Hill there which reminds them of certain things. They had a James Otis there, and to him will history certainly award the merit of having inaugurated the doctrines of the Revolutionary war.

Sir, I said yesterday that I could not suppose that anybody believed that the Republican party differed with the old men of the Confederation, who passed the ordinance of 1787, at the very time they were making the Constitution. I do not think any man on the other side, or any side, or anywhere in the world, can say to me that I differ with the founders of the Republic, that I differ with the men who made the Constitution, on this subject. Why so? I say that I agree with them. My principle is to exclude forced labor—negro labor—from every Territory where white men can work well and be healthy. That is my idea. But I do not know but that I shall be turned out of the Republican party by my friend from Illinois [Mr. LOVEJOY] for heresy. That is my doctrine, and I say that the founders of the Constitution and of the Republic had that very idea, and put it into practice by excluding slavery, in 1787, from the entire Northwestern Territory, now five powerful States. I now pass to the question of the *power* of the Congress of the United States. If the men of 1787 were right in their policy, then I think that every gentleman will say that we are equally right in entertaining similar views. If the men of former times had the truth with them in saying that it was better, not alone for the present States, not for the East, nor for the West, not for the North, nor for the South, alone, but for all of them; better for the whole Republic, that the white children of the father should go to a place where they could work well and be healthy; better for these and better for all, that the children of the white man should have all that unoccupied land, if not too hot for them—if they believed that they were *right* in that, then I say we will find power in the Constitution, if we by fair construction can, to do *that right* thing. I think that I have established the point, at least, that the Republican party proposes to do exactly that which the makers of the Constitution did, a year before the Constitution was made. They got the power to do it under the old Confederation; they had that power, not merely by the consent of the South, but at the urgent request of the South. Now, have we the power under the Constitution to do it?

The gentleman from Mississippi [Mr. LAMAR] suggested to me yesterday that the law organizing the Territory of Orleans recognised slavery there. So it did. I wish, now, that section of the law enacted in 1798, for the government of the Territory of Mississippi, be read.

The Clerk read, as follows:

"SEC. 7. *And be it further enacted*, That from 'and after the establishment of the aforesaid 'Government, it shall not be lawful for any per- 'son or persons to import or bring into the said 'Mississippi Territory, from any port or place 'without the limits of the United States, or to 'cause or procure to be so imported or brought, 'or knowingly to aid or assist in so importing or 'bringing, any slave or slaves; and that every 'person so offending, and being thereof con- 'victed before any court within said Territory, 'having competent jurisdiction, shall forfeit and 'pay, for each and every slave so imported or 'brought, the sum of $300; one moiety for the 'use of the United States, and the other moiety 'for the use of any person or persons who shall 'sue for the same; and that every slave so im- 'ported or brought shall thereupon become en- 'titled to, and receive, his or her freedom."

I have read that section of the law. Now, Mr. Clerk, to show that at that time, in 1798, the Congress of the United States assumed and exercised a power in a Territory which they were forbidden by the Constitution to exercise towards a State, is proof conclusive that they at that time understood that they had the power to make laws concerning slavery and the slave trade in the Territories.

There are some other matters, sir, which I have been looking at this morning, which I wish also to read. About the year 1808, a gentleman whom some of us remember well, being then a Delegate from the Territory of Mississippi, (Mr. Poindexter,) moved to change the organic law of that Territory, so that the Governor should not have the power of proroguing the Legislature at his pleasure. Then, as is usual in deliberative bodies, a discussiou sprung up upon general questions involved. On that occasion a gentleman from Georgia, whom I had also the pleasure to know for some time—a Mr. Troup—made the following remarks:

"By the articles of cession, the right of soil 'and jurisdiction was ceded to the people of the 'United States on the express condition that the 'articles of the ordinance should form the gov- 'ernment of the Mississippi Territory, and that 'they should not be governed otherwise. The 'inference inevitably is, that the State of 'Georgia would not have ceded but upon the ex- 'press condition; and this inference is the more 'inevitable, inasmuch as in this clause Georgia 'has made an express exception to a particular 'article in the ordinance; from which I say that 'Georgia intended that no other alteration should 'be made.

"What was the policy of the ordinance, and 'what the object of its framers? Why, assured- 'ly, to render the Government of the Territories 'dependent upon the Government of the United 'States. And how was it to be effected? By 'making the Territorial Legislature in a great 'degree dependent on the Governor, and him 'absolutely dependent on the Federal Executive. 'The moment we make the Legislature of a Ter- 'ritory independent of its Executive, we make it 'independent of the Federal Government." * *

"But the gentleman from Mississippi Territory 'is certainly mistaken as to one point. He 'seems to consider the Constitution of the Uni- 'ted States as giving to the people of the Territo- 'ries the same rights as the people of the States. 'It is a mistaken idea, neither warranted by the 'letter or the spirit of the Constitution; for 'although the Constitution has declared that the 'people of one State are entitled to all the rights 'and privileges of another, yet it has not de- 'clared that the people of the Territories have 'the same rights as the people of the States. 'In another part of the Constitution, it is indeed 'expressly declared that Congress shall make 'all laws for the disposal of the Territories; but 'there is a salvo that all acts done and contracts 'made previous to the adoption of the Constitu- 'tion shall be as binding as if done afterward. 'The articles of the ordinance were enacted pre- 'viously, and are consequently binding under 'the Constitution. It cannot be controverted 'that they were wisely adopted, and have been 'salutary in their operation. They were framed 'by the Congress of 1787, composed of men 'whose integrity was incorruptible and judg- 'ment almost infallible. These articles, from 'that time to this, have remained unaltered, and 'carried the Territories, through difficulties 'almost insuperable, to prosperity. And now, 'for the first or second time, an alteration is 'proposed, the consequence of which cannot be 'foreseen, without any evidence that it is either 'necessary or expedient.

"The population of every new country must 'necessarily be composed of a heterogeneous 'mixture of various tempers, characters, and in- 'terests. In a population thus composed, it 'would be highly ridiculous to expect that love 'of order and obedience to law would always 'predominate. Therefore the old Congress 'wisely reserved to itself the right to control 'them; to give the Governor power, when a 'Legislature became disorderly, to dissolve them; 'and for the exercise of this power he is account- 'able to the General Government.

"The gentleman from Mississippi wishes us 'not to treat the Territories as children, whose 'wild extravagances may require correcting 'by the indulgent hand of their parents, but 'as the equals of the States, without any other 'reason than that which he states to be the sit- 'uation of the people of his Territory. They 'will next wish us to admit them into the Union 'before their population will authorize it; tell 'us that that Territory does not grow fast 'enough, and we must demolish the system for 'their convenience."

Mr. Clerk, it will be observed that, in all the early discussions about the power of Congress in relation to a Territory, it has been admitted that Congress had entire control over its legislation under the Constitution of the United States. I would, if I thought it prudent, commend to my Illinois friends and to others, who contend for this very plausible and captivating doctrine of popular sovereignty in the Territories, to examine what it was the great founders of the Republic thought on that subject. I would advise them, as the honest clergymen of Illinois, who are about to be silenced by some law which we hear of, would do: to give it their prayerful attention. [Laughter.]

I now send to the Clerk's desk, to be read, the tenth section of a law passed in 1804, to be enforced in the *Territory* of Orleans, which was thereby established.

The Clerk read, as follows:

"Sec. 10. It shall not be lawful for any per- 'son or persons to import or bring into the said 'Territory, from any port or place *without the 'limits of the United States*, or cause or procure 'to be so imported or brought, or knowingly 'to aid or assist in importing or bringing, any 'slave or slaves; and every person so offending, 'and being thereof convicted before any court 'within said Territory having competent juris- 'diction, shall forfeit and pay, for each and 'every slave so imported or brought, the sum 'of $300, one moiety for the use of the United 'States, and the other moiety for the use of the 'person or persons who shall sue for the same; and 'every slave so imported or brought shall there- 'upon become entitled to and receive his or her 'freedom. It shall not be lawful for any person 'or persons to import or bring into the said 'Territory, from any port or place within the 'limits of the United States, or to cause or pro- 'cure to be so imported or brought, or knowingly 'to aid or assist in so importing or bringing, any 'slave or slaves which shall have been imported 'since the 1st day of May, 1798, into any port or 'place within the limits of the United States, or 'which may hereafter be so imported from any 'port or place without the limits of the United 'States; and every person so offending, and be- 'ing thereof convicted before any court within 'said Territory having competent jurisdiction, 'shall forfeit and pay for each and every slave so 'imported or brought from without the United 'States the sum of $300, one moiety for the use 'of the United States, and the other moiety for 'the use of the person or persons who shall sue 'for the same; and no slave or slaves shall, 'directly or indirectly, be introduced into said 'Territory, *except by a citizen of the United States 'removing into said Territory for actual settlement, 'and being, at the time of such removal, bona fide 'owner of such slave or slaves;* and every slave 'imported or brought into the said Territory con- 'trary to the provisions of this act shall there-

'upon be entitled to and receive his or her free-'dom."

Mr. Clerk, I do not have these extracts read from the early legislation of the Congress of the United States, regarding this matter, with any view now to enter into an argument showing that they were constitutional. I only produce them as the *opinions of the men of that day*, and which heretofore have been considered safe counsellors on questions of constitutional law. What they did certainly evinces their belief that they had power to regulate the question of slavery in Territories. I wish now to commend to the consideration of the House, on this point, the opinions of another gentleman, (Mr. Louis McLane,) long known and deservedly honored in the legislative and executive annals of the country; always considered as exalting in his person the executive offices he occupied; a foreign minister of the very highest reputation since the old men of the revolutionary time have passed away. His son is now one of the diplomatic agents of the country. Mr. Louis McLane said what I send to the Clerk.

The Clerk read, as follows:

"Mr. Chairman, the people of Missouri cannot 'be incorporated into the Union but as the people 'of a 'State,' exercising State government. It is 'a union of States, not of people, much less of Territories. A Territorial Government can 'form no integral part of a union of State Gov-'ernments; neither can the people of a Territory 'enjoy any Federal rights until they have formed 'a State Government and obtained admission 'into the Union. The most important of the 'Federal advantages and immunities consist in 'the right of being represented in Congress—as 'well in the Senate as in this House—the right 'of participating in the councils by which they 'are governed. These are emphatically the 'rights, advantages, and immunities, of citizens 'of the United States.' The inhabitant of a 'Territory merely has no such rights. He is not 'a citizen of the United States. He is in a state 'of disability as it respects his political or civil 'rights. Can it be called a 'right' to acquire 'and hold property, and have no voice by which 'its disposition is to be regulated? Can it be 'called an advantage or immunity of a citizen 'of the United States to be subjected to a Gov-'ernment in whose deliberations he has no share 'or agency beyond the mere arbitrary pleasure 'of the Governor—to be ruled by a power ir-'responsible (to him, at least) for its conduct? 'Sir, the rights, advantages, and immunities, of 'citizens of the United States, and which are 'their proudest boast, are the rights of self-'government—first, in their State Constitu-'tions; and secondly, in the Government of the 'Union, in which they have an equal participa-'tion." * * *

"The right to govern a Territory is clearly in-'cident to the right of acquiring it. It would be 'absurd to say that any Government might pur-chase a Territory with a population, and not 'have the power to give them laws; but, from 'whatever source the power is derivable, I admit 'it to be plenary, so long as it remains in a con-'dition of Territorial dependence, but no longer. 'I am willing at any time to exercise this power. 'I regret that it has not been done sooner. *But, 'though Congress can give laws to a Territory*, it 'cannot prescribe them to a State. *The condition 'of the people of a Territory is to be governed by 'others; of a State, to govern themselves."—Annals 'of Sixteenth Congress, First Session, vol.* 1, *pages* '1145, 1146, 1160.

The general drift of all these observations of the early men of the country concedes the fact that when a Territory is acquired, it is, before it becomes a State, to be governed by the Congress of the United States, whether you derive that power from the clause of the Constitution which says Congress shall have power to make all needful rules and regulations respecting the territory and other property of the United States, or derive it as an incident to the power to make war, as some contend, or as incident to the power to make treaties without qualification, as others contend. You see that the power to make laws for a Territory was always considered, under one or the other of these clauses, as belonging to Congress. As that power is without limitation—as there is no possible limitation placed on it by these views of the subject—I maintain that it is just as large a legislative power as the States have in regulating their State policy. I hold, and I may differ from some of my Republican friends, that Congress can enact that slavery shall be in a Territory, or enact that it shall not be in a Territory, just as fully and freely as a State can do the same within its limits.

Let us now recur for a few moments to the legislation of Congress in that portion of the Louisiana purchase lying north of latitude 36° 30′—that part of the purchase now known as Kansas and Nebraska. I was endeavoring to show that the Cabinet of Mr. Monroe had all, upon mature reflection, in 1821, conceded the power of Congress to prohibit slavery in a Territory, as they did in that Missouri restriction. When I quoted the opinions of Mr. Calhoun, it was suggested by the gentleman from South Carolina [Mr. KEITT] that Mr. Calhoun did not approve of it at the time. I have in my hand an extract from a speech of Mr. Calhoun, delivered in the Senate in 1838, when that question came directly before that body. I had, I thought, a very perfect recollection of it; but I did not like to state it positively yesterday. It was made in a debate upon a resolution which he himself had offered, in which he said that any attempt by Congress to abolish slavery in the District of Columbia, upon the ground that it was sinful, would be a dangerous invasion of the rights of the South. He went further, and said that Congress had no right to determine whether the institutions of a State were wicked or righteous. I am very much of that opinion myself. I think every State has sins enough to answer for itself, without interfering with its neighbors. When that subject was under discussion, Mr. Calhoun said:

"He was gald that the portion of the amend-'ment which referred to the Missouri compromise 'had been struck out. He was not a member of

'Congress when that compromise was made, but 'it is due to candor to state that his impressions 'were in its favor; but it is equally due to it to 'say that, with his present experience and 'knowledge of the spirit which then, for the first 'time, began to disclose itself, he had entirely 'changed his opinion."

This is from Mr. Calhoun's own speech, made in 1838. I read from Benton's Thirty Years in the United States Senate, page 136.* It was made in a very animated discussion, which was conducted with perfect propriety and gentlemanly deportment, but with zeal and fervor and great power, too—all of which contributes to the usefulness of every discussion; and which I could wish, in common with us all, might be more sedulously imitated by us all upon this floor, in this present House of Representatives.

Now, I could read further, if cumulative testimony were wanting to show that Mr. Calhoun was in favor of that law. I think I have shown that the whole Cabinet did agree to it; and I only now wish to show that they agreed to it deliberately and in writing. Mr. Benton, on page 141 of the same work, has collected, among other proofs, the following:

"First, a *fac simile* copy of an original paper in 'Mr. Monroe's handwriting, found among his 'manuscript papers, dated March 4, 1820, (two 'days before the approval of the Missouri com-'promise act,) and endorsed: 'Interrogatories—'Missouri—to the Heads of Departments and the 'Attorney General,' and containing within two 'questions:

"1. Has Congress a right, under the powers 'vested in it by the Constitution, to make a reg-'ulation prohibiting slavery in a Territory.

"2. Is the eighth section of the act which pass-'ed both houses of Congress on the 3d instant, 'for the admission of Missouri into the Union, 'consistent with the Constitution?"

This is a letter in the handwriting of Mr. Monroe, and the endorsement, as I have said, is in his handwriting; and it was made two days before the act making this restriction was approved by him as President. The second piece of testimony collected here is:

"The draft of an orignal letter in Mr. Monroe's 'handwriting, but without signature, date, or 'address, but believed to have been a copy of a 'letter addressed to General Jackson, in which 'he says:

"'The question which lately agitated Con-'gress and the public has been settled, as you 'have seen, by the passage of an act for the ad-'mission of Missouri as a State, unrestricted; 'and Arkansas also, when it reaches maturity; 'and the establishment of the parallel of 36° '30′ as a line north of which slavery is prohib-'ited, and permitted south of it. *I took the opin-'ion, in writing, of the Administration, as to the con-'stitutionality of restraining Territories, which was 'explicit in favor of it; and it was, that the eighth 'section of the act was applicable to Territories only,* 'and not to States when they should be admit-'ted into the Union.'"

The third piece of testimony collected by Mr. Benton is:

"An extract from the diary of Mr. John 'Quincy Adams, under date of the 3d of March, '1821, stating that the President on that day as-'sembled his Cabinet, to ask their opinions on 'the two questions mentioned, which the whole 'Cabinet immediately answered *unanimously* and '*affirmatively*; that, on the 5th, he sent the ques-'tion in writing to the members of his Cabinet, 'to receive their written answers, to be filed in 'the Department of State; and that, on the 6th, 'he took his own answer to the President, to be 'filed with the rest—all agreeing in the affirma-'tive, and only differing, some in assigning, 'others not assigning, reasons for their opin-'ions. The diary states that the President signed 'his approval of the Missouri act on the 6th, '[which act shows he did,] and requested Mr. 'Adams to have all the opinions filed in the De-'partment of State."

The other day, some gentleman upon the other side of the House read that diary, as extracted from Mr. Adams's journal. Mr. Benton only condenses it, and all will agree that it is correctly stated here. After that, in 1855, a letter was addressed by Mr. Benton to Mr. Clayton, who was Secretary of State in 1849–'50, to know what had become of these written opinions. Mr. Clayton answered, under date of July 19, 1855, as follows:

"In reply to your inquiry, I have to state that 'I have no recollection of having ever met with 'Mr. Calhoun's answer to Mr. Monroe's Cabinet 'queries as to the constitutionality of the Mis-'souri compromise. It had not been found while 'I was in the Department of State, as I was then 'informed; but the archives of the Department 'disclose the fact that Mr. Calhoun, and other 'members of the Cabinet, did answer Mr. Mon-'roe's questions. It appears, by an index, that 'these answers were filed among the archives of 'that Department. I was told that they had 'been abstracted from the records, and could not 'be found; but I did not make a search for them 'myself. I have never doubted that Mr. Calhoun 'at least acquiesced in the decision of the Cab-'inet of that day. Since I left the Department 'of State, I have heard it rumored that Mr. Cal-'houn's answer to Mr. Monroe's queries had 'been found; but I know not upon what author-'ity the statement was made."

I think, Mr. Clerk, that if we were in a court of justice, and before a jury, with the fact in dispute whether Mr. Monroe's Cabinet did make these answers affirmatively, and if I were maintaining the affirmative of that proposition, I should be sure to get the unanimous verdict of a sensible jury on that point, on the evidence. I shall therefore assume it as true, as a matter of history, that, in the year 1821, James Monroe, President of the United States; John Quincy

* Mr. Lamar, of Mississippi, between whom and Mr. Corwin there was a colloquy as to the correctness of Mr. Benton's citation, seemed to doubt that Mr. Calhoun had ever made such an admission. The extract here given will be found in Mr. Calhoun's remarks in the Senate, on the —— day of 1838, during the debate on his celebrated resolutions on slavery, precisely as Mr. Benton quotes in the "Thirty Years View."—*See Appendix Congressional Globe, Second Session Twenty-fifth Congress, vol. 6, page 72.*

Adams, Secretary of State; William H. Crawford, Secretary of the Treasury; John C. Calhoun, Secretary of War; Smith Thompson, Secretary of the Navy; William Wirt, Attorney General, all agreed, after hearing that debate—going on, as it had been, for two years in Congress—with their minds imbued with all the arguments on both sides, came to the conclusion that Congress did possess, always had possessed, and always would possess, the unqualified power to restrict slavery in the Territories, or to make any other law they pleased on the subject. That is all the sin the Republican party has committed. I believe that Mr. Monroe did know something about the Constitution of the country. I believe that John Quincy Adams did understand something of the nature of this delicate machinery of ours, as it is now called. The Republican party is weak enough to believe that there are some men in the world who have brains in their heads besides themselves. They believe the men of 1821, as well as the great men of 1787 and 1804, all held the doctrines of the Republican party of 1860; and this, I think, I have proved.

Sir, need I now call from their homes in eternity the great and good men who, in 1787, declared that it was not just or politic to permit slavery in the territory northwest of the Ohio, and so ordained? Need I call the shades of Monroe and his Cabinet from the "abodes of the blessed," to come here into this Hall, and declare again, in the presence of the world, the same doctrines they have declared under just such obligations as now rest upon us? I could wish that this majestic and venerated host could pass in review before the vision of the Democratic members here this day. Each and all would range themselves on the Republican side of this House; for there, and there only, in this House, would they find the principles, policy, and constitutional law, which they proclaimed, acted upon, and established, from the day they broke the yoke of foreign power up to the day when it pleased God to relieve them from their earthly trials, and take them to himself.

Mr. Clerk, I find myself at a loss to understand how it is possible for the gentlemen on the other side to rid their minds of the crushing weight of authority which presses against them, upon this subject, either as to the policy of restricting slavery, or the power of Congress to do it. Will they assert that the men of 1787 were mistaken in the policy, and that Congress and the Executive department, from 1804 to 1821, were mistaken in the point of constitutional power? Where is the enormous egotist to be found who will assert that *he* understands, to-day, the Constitution of the United States better than President Monroe and his entire Cabinet did in 1821?

Monroe was a patriot and a soldier of the Revolution. He was familiar with all the deliberations of the wise men and all the thoughts and writings of his times which led to the formation of the Union and the adoption of the Constitution. He was an anxious participant in the discussions concerning the powers vested in Congress by that Constitution. He had carefully watched its operations from the time of its adoption up to 1821, when he was called upon, under the responsibilities resting on the highest officer of the Government, to decide whether Congress possessed the power to prohibit slavery in a "*Territory*." He was a Virginian, a slaveholder; and, if biassed at all, that bias might be expected to incline him against the power. Such a man, such a President, on full deliberation, decided that such power did exist in, and by virtue of, that Constitution, and accordingly approved the act of Congress which exerted that power. John Quincy Adams was his Secretary of State. A child of the Revolution, educated in the principles which brought that Revolution to its glorious conclusion, thoroughly taught and studied in the science of jurisprudence, he brought to this very question all the powers of a mind naturally strong, strengthened and enriched by all the appliances of study, while its operations were freed from all sinister influences, by candor and integrity which even party malignity has never questioned. Adams was a Northern man, and not a slaveholder. He, too, agreed with Monroe, the Southern slaveholder. William H. Crawford, of Georgia, was then the Secretary of the Treasury. He was a Southern man, and a slaveholder. He was at that time a most notable man among men who were indeed worthy of notice—a man of austere virtues, and yet of kindly and generous nature. But, above almost all men of his time, he was remarkable and remarked for carrying what is called "strict construction" to great extremes. Every power not clearly granted, in terms, to the Federal Government, was, by him and his school, denied to the Government and reserved to the States or the people; and this, too, whether such power were claimed for the executive, or legislative, or judicial department. In this characteristic he stood in perfect contrast with his colleague in the War Department, Mr. Calhoun, who then held doctrines on this subject condemned by Mr. Crawford and his school as dangerous, as latitudinarian. Mr. Crawford had been much in public life; had studied—as men of that day did—the Constitution, and all other forms of civil polity found in libraries accessible to them. His name and character will long live in the esteem of all Georgians, as well as in that of all Americans who venerate the wise and good. Crawford, strict constructionist as he was, slaveholder as he was, admitted that Congress had power to prohibit slavery in a Territory. John C. Calhoun was also in this Cabinet council of 1821.* He was then Secretary of War. He was a South Carolinian, and a slaveholder; a man of rare powers of mind, quick in discerning the point of merit in any question. His power of "generalization" was greater and more rapid in its processes than that of any man with whom I have had the good fortune to be acquainted. All Southern as he was, he, too, admitted this power to subsist in Congress; and, as I think I have shown, gave his written opinion to that effect under all the grave responsibilities of a "Cabinet minister." Smith Thompson, of New York, was then Secretary of the Navy. This gentleman is better known to the world as a Judge of the Supreme Court of the

United States, to which place he was transferred on account of his accurate and profound knowledge of law—law as a science—comprehending all subjects embraced in what are denominated national and municipal law. He was a Northern man, and to the four others I have enumerated he added the great weight of his opinion, concurring with them fully and entirely.

But who was he, the then Attorney General of that Cabinet?—he whose entire official duty it was to advise the President and each one of the Cabinet on questions of law? Mr. Wirt was that Attorney General—a name known and respected by all lawyers who know anything of law; a name equally known and respected by all, of all classes and professions, who admire true intellectual greatness combined with amenity of manners and amiability of temper that won the affections of all hearts; a man of such rich and diversified intellect, that while he toiled in the profoundest depths of the richest mines of legal learning, yet found leisure and had the taste to gather from the gardens of polite letters some of the richest and rarest of their fruits and flowers; and, to crown all, he was gifted with an eloquence that charmed and enraptured all who heard him. To this Virginian, this slaveholder, this all-accomplished mind, our Republican platform of this day was submitted. It was not then a great spring-board whence some insane aspirant for Presidential power was to leap into the coveted Executive chair; it was not then a principle to be used only for the occasion, and to be announced to the world amid the hoarse clamor of popular strife, and then abandoned at the end of four years for some novelty more captivating to the popular ear. It was argued, considered, and decided, by such men as I have named, at a time when the old party names, Federalist and Republican, had ceased to have a meaning; when the beacon fires of party war were quenched in the pure waters of a pervading American patriotism.

As the Republican platform (so much derided and condemned *now* by learned gentlemen of the Democratic party) now reads, so did the great tribunal to which I am now referring decide the law of the Constitution. To this august court I appeal, from the hasty opinions of your modern politicians and the teachings and paragraphs cut from obscure newspapers. To that tribunal I summon, for judgment and sentence of death, these *new* notions which teach us that this same Constitution, which in 1821 permitted Congress to forbid slavery in "*Territories,*" now, in 1860, tramples Congress and its power, scoffs at all power, Federal or Territorial, and bears slavery, as the phrase goes, "*suo proprio vigore,*" into all Territories; and only pauses to bow with royal courtesy to the crowned and sceptred majesty of State Constitutions. Hither, also, do I summon that other modern partisan war-cry, "popular sovereignty," born of the partisan struggles of 1854. From the heated furnaces of political strife, this fire went forth. It shed its baleful light over Kansas for three troubled years; blazed up to noon-tide, and then, like a tropical sun, dashed down the sky, cast a lurid blaze over the chaos it had created, and sunk, quenched in blood, leaving behind it only the spectral images of confusion and war which its brief day had evoked into life.

Mr. Clerk, in treating this subject of the power of Congress over Territories, the object of our inquiry is to ascertain whether any clause in the Constitution gives, in terms or by fair implication, the power in question. In all such cases the inquiry is, what is the true intent and meaning of the Constitution? The words employed are to be carefully criticized; and if they be *plainly* such as to give or deny the power, then the meaning is ascertained. If doubts arise, however, from an examination of the words employed, it is always safe to ascertain, in other modes, what they did mean who wrote and enacted these words. Hence, the acts of individuals, done in performance of their own written engagements, show what they understood their own written contracts to mean. So the conduct of nations in the execution of treaties is always resorted to to show what each nation understood its treaty contracts to bind it to perform. This plain rule of good sense, when applied to Constitutions or legislative enactments, is called "cotemporaneous construction."

Sir, we know that while the Convention that formed the Constitution was in session, in the year 1787, the old Congress, under the old Articles of Confederation, passed the celebrated ordinance of 1787, whereby that Congress did enact that there should be "no slavery or involuntary servitude" in the then Northwestern Territory. It is only reasonable to suppose that the Convention then in session, seeing this power exerted by Congress under the old Government, should conclude that the same ought to be granted to Congress in the *new* Constitution, which was to supersede the old "Confederation." Accordingly we find a clause inserted, which says:

"Congress shall have power to make all needful rules and '*regulations*' concerning the territory and other property of the United States."

The men who enacted the ordinance of 1787, and those who formed the Constitution, were many of them the same persons. Is it not an irresistible conclusion that they did intend, by the clause I have quoted, to confer the same power upon Congress by that clause which they had in the old Congress, in the same year, themselves exerted, by virtue of the powers given to Congress by the "Articles of Confederation," under which they then acted? Let us not be told that the power "*to make all needful rules and regulations concerning* the territory," was inserted in haste, or was not well examined and well understood. Before the Constitution was adopted, and after it was formed, it underwent the closest scrutiny. The public prints teemed with criticisms upon all its provisions. State Conventions debated it with all the interest its vast importance naturally elicited, and with all the power which the greatest minds, in that age of truly great men, could bring to the discussion. They knew the meaning and import of every word, and the extent and intent of every power granted to each branch of the new Government. Now, we also know that the leading men in the Convention that formed this Constitution were many of them leading and active men in the legislative, judicial, and executive departments of the Government under this Constitution. In every office they may have thus held, they took a solemn oath to "observe the Constitution," it being the same they themselves had made. We must admit, therefore, that *they* did not intend to violate any clause in that Constitution. Even the Democratic party will not assert that the great men to that day would be likely to commit perjury, and, in doing it, destroy their own great work; for all of them regarded the Union under that Constitution as furnishing the only hope remaining to them and their posterity, of realizing their long-cherished object, rational freedom regulated by law. Did not they think they had the constitutional power to do that? They did it in 1798; they did it in 1804; they did it in 1820. These were fathers of the Revolution; the apostles were there, making their own commentary upon their own gospel; and this was the commentary: that Congress make laws for the territory, composed as it was of a heterogeneous and discordant population, not likely to agree among themselves upon any system of civil polity. We treat them as infants. We, owning the country, are the proper legislative power to give it laws. That is the way they treated it; and I never shall believe that they intended that that power should not be there when they made the Constitution. If they had not intended it to be there, they never would have exerted it. They would have asked for an amendment of the Constitution if they had thought it necessary; but they went right forward, and exerted the power, because they knew the power to be there. One of two conclusions you must come to, or admit the full weight of my authorities: either that these men violated the Constitution which they had sworn to support, knowingly and wilfully, or that they, the makers and cotemporaneous exponents of the Constitution, did conscientiously believe that it gave them this power. Who knows so well what he meant to do, what he meant to say, and what he meant to inculcate, as the author of the book himself? And if he be honest, he will always give you the true meaning. Thus we have this constitutional gospel delivered to us by no remote posterity, not acquainted with the writers; by no commentator or historian at all; but by the fathers, the very men themselves who wrote the book. And we, of the Republican party, are to be charged with treason, and with an odious attempt to disrupt this glorious Union which these very men made for us; we are to be denounced for believing these opinions to be right, instead of believing the doctrines of modern commentators on that Constitution, who have found out that the authors of it did not know what they meant!

Now we have got through with the legislative and executive history of this Constitution of ours. I was stating yesterday what the Supreme Court had done. A friend of mine has been kind enough to furnish me with a speech made by a gentleman in the Senate, who has collected the very authorities to which I wanted to refer. From that I shall read to show what the judiciary think about this matter. As I said yesterday, such is the structure of our Government, that, if there be any dispute about the constitutional power of Congress in making a law, and an individual right comes in question, so as to give the judicial department of the Government cognizance of it, and they decide that the law is unconstitutional, I know of no relief against that decision, if it shall be wrong.

I wish to show what the judicial department of the Government thought of this power of Congress to govern the Territories. There is a case referred to which I had not before me yesterday, and I have been unable to get the book from the Library this morning. I take it for granted that it is here correctly referred to, and that the quotations are correct. It is the case of Sere *vs.* Pitot. It occurred in 1810, and is reported in 6 Cranch, page 336. The Supreme Court of the United States, without a dissenting voice, in the most explicit language, then declared "that the 'power of governing and legislating for a Territory is the inevitable consequence of the right 'to acquire and hold it."

Let me advert to that Supreme Court. Who were upon the bench of the Supreme Court at that day? Look at the judicial records of the country. There was John Marshall, and all of them like him in great qualities of mind and nature. Virginians know who I mean when I refer to John Marshall. Questions are not brought up in that court as they are here. A gentleman jumps up in the morning here to set himself right before the country. [Laughter.] To do that, he offers a resolution. The House votes on it. One gentleman speaks over on that side, and another gentleman speaks on this side, pretty nearly all the time he has the floor. Fifty gentlemen sit between, engaged in an earnest colloquy as to what the speakers are saying. [Laughter.] It is to be inferred that we have a fair opportunity of knowing the opinions of gentlemen. That is the way we decide great questions here at this time in our present unorganized condition. Go into the Supreme Court. Not a whisper is heard. The court is opened, and sits for four hours. You might, at the time I refer to, have argued a question for three weeks, if you had the power to hold out so long, and every judge would have been found listening every day and every hour and every minute. All the learning of the law, all the history of the law, all the logic of the law, is laid before that court; and the court, accustomed to look into the intricacies of the law, will revolve all that has been brought before them in their minds, and pronounce what is and what is not law. They have sober and discreet minds. It is a better court than this. I do not mean to cast any disparagement upon your court, Mr. Clerk. I wish, if it could be so, that from the beginning of this session the Journal clerk had every night blotted out the record of our proceedings, that they might not be heard of any more among men. When I entered this Hall a new man the other day, there was a strange feeling came upon me that I was not in the Congress of the United States. Over the chair where the Speaker presided sat, in the old time, the Muse of History, with her pen. The men who built the first Hall of the House of Representatives thought that this grand inquest of this great Republic was to make that history which should illustrate our annals. Clio was there, emblematical of what was to be submitted to the dread tribunal of posterity.

But to the decision of the court. The decision referred to is to be found in 6 Cranch, page 336. There was no dissenting opinion. It was in 1810. There was no Democratic party in those days; but there was a Republican party. This question was not decided the year before a Presidential election. Time is always a circumstance to be looked at in referring to a historical fact. There was then a powerful party in this country called the Republican party, and there was a remnant of an old and most respectable party called Federalists; and they were discussing whether we should make war upon England or upon France. I have always thought they were not sure which one of these nations to fight; and that they were never sure they had hit upon the right one; for they had quite equal causes of war against both. They recollected La Fayette was with us, and that, I believe, turned the scales against England. Says the court of that day:

"The power of governing and legislating for a 'Territory is the inevitable consequence of the 'right to acquire and hold territory. Could this 'position be contested, the Constitution declares 'that 'Congress shall have power to dispose of 'and make all needful rules and regulations re-'specting the territory or other property belong-'ing to the United States;' accordingly, we find 'Congress possessing and exercising the absolute 'and undisputed power of governing and legisla-'ting for the Territory of Orleans."

Do you not think, Mr. Clerk, that John Marshall was a man who knew and understood the subject then before him? If any question could be submitted to the mind of that man with which he was more familiar than any other, it was a question arising under the powers of the Government as defined in that Constitution. We know that the whole court agreed with him in 1810. I have shown the legislative history of this question. Now, it was declared by the Supreme Court, as early as 1810, that the power to govern the Territories arises under the power to acquire territory, or under the clause of the Constitution authorizing Congress to make all needful rules and regulations respecting the territory and other property of the United States. So much for 1810. Now, some years have elapsed. In 1 Peters, page 511, there is a reference to the same question, and the law is laid down in the same terms as in 1810. In the mean time, says Judge Marshall, "Florida continues to be a Territory of the Uni-'ted States, governed by that clause of the Con-'stitution which empowers Congress to make all 'needful rules and regulations respecting the ter-'ritory or other property of the United States." He goes on:

"Perhaps the power of governing a Territory 'belonging to the United States, which has not, 'by becoming a State, acquired the means of 'self-government, may result necessarily from 'the facts that it is not within the jurisdiction 'of any particular State, and is within the power 'and jurisdiction of the United States. The 'right to govern may be the inevitable con-'sequence of the right to acquire territory. 'Whichever may be the source whence the 'power may be derived, the possession of it is 'unquestioned."

These Republican traitors, these dupes, these insurrectionists, these one hundred and thirteen men who were, as you say, by intendment, at Harper's Ferry with John Brown; these men have committed no sin but that of believing, with Judge Marshall, and with the Supreme Court up to the year 1828, in the opinions they entertain. I shall show, by and by, that the same doctrine now held by the Republican party was carried forward by an unbroken current of decisions up to the year 1852.

Much is said by the present Democratic party *just now* about the sanctity of constitutional law, as delivered to us by the Supreme Court. I revere that great court, and will abide its decisions, when made upon any question brought fairly on the record before them; which, I maintain, was not done, as some suppose, in the famous Dred Scott case. Gentlemen on the other side would disregard the solemn decisions of that court for half a century, and cling to an *obiter dictum*, casually thrown out in a single case recently. They remind me of a dispute between two excellent clergymen. They both regarded the Old and New Testaments very properly as the oracles of God; but they differed as to their meaning. "Well, brother," said the old Methodist, "we agree well enough about the Adamic law and the Abrahamic covenant, and the Divine legation of Moses; but when we come to the Christian dispensation, you will fork off." Our Democratic brethren here have a strange disposition to "fork off" from us, and run after the casual remarks of the court—the "*obiter dicta*" of the court, to express it in judicial phrase—while they travel on with us in the well-paved highway up to 1852.

Mr. Clerk, I know that this long, wandering journey among the legislative annals and judicial records of the country, is very tedious; but truth is a jewel of such precious value, that we are told we must go to the bottom of a deep well after it, if, perchance, we may find it there. I wish to let down my pitcher for another draught of that sort of water from the well of the Supreme Court. Two decisions of that court we have had already. Here is the third in the year 1853. We are coming now close upon the period of the Democratic Hegira. In 1853, a very few weeks before the introduction of the Kansas-Nebraska bill, there was an opinion pronounced by Judge Wayne, at the December term of that court, in which he said:

"The Territory [speaking of California] had 'been ceded as a conquest, and was to be pre-'served and governed as such, until the sove-

'reignty to which it passed [the United States] 'had legislated for it."

He proceeds:

"That sovereignty was the United States, un- 'der the Constitution, by which power had been 'given to Congress 'to dispose of and make all 'needful rules and regulations respecting the 'territory or other property belonging to the 'United States.'"

Then, I say, from the earliest period of our Government down to 1853, everybody—all agreeing to it; all shades of politics; Congresses of every hue of politics; all the courts of the country, all over it—regarded the question as clearly settled, as the Republicans now hold it. I wish this speech of mine, so far as it goes, imperfect as it is, to be considered as "Corwin's Apology for Republicanism." Mr. Barclay wrote "An Apology for Quakerism," a capital book, with a good deal of sense in it. My Apology for Republicanism may not be quite as authoritative.

What I have proved, I think to the satisfaction of all, is, that the men who framed the Constitution acted upon the power to govern the Territories, believing it to be there; and they acted under oath; that the legislative department of the Government always have exercised it up to the year 1854; and that the judicial department of the Government decided the law thus, whenever the question arose, up to the year 1853. Now, I say to gentlemen upon the other side, if you can put yourself in as good society as this Republican party are in, then I will agree to pay a visit to you, and perhaps stay all night. [Laughter.] Until you do, I choose to put up at the Republican hotel. [Laughter.] I wish to compare graveyards, monuments, epitaphs, and authorities, with the Democratic party. We Republicans may possibly be under a great mistake upon this subject; but if we are, the most intelligent people, according to your own account of it—and I believe it true—have been under the same mistake from the beginning.

Sir, I am an old Whig; and the very doctrines which the Whig party always inculcated upon this subject are the cardinal doctrines of the Republican party; and the only constitutional doctrines they have enunciated were born of a violation of the same Whig doctrines in 1854. The Republican party had never had a name, and never had an existence, in that form and that name, had it not been for the proceedings of that Congress in 1854. I suppose that every man will admit this. And why? Why was that treasonable party, as you now denominate it, brought into existence? Do you suppose that all the people of the North are insane? I would like an inquest of lunacy to try the question, and I would show where the insanity is. It was in that year 1854 that you proposed to renounce this doctrine of the control of Congress over the Territories. It was then that you determined to depart from that compromise of 1850, to which my friend from Illinois [Mr. McClernand] just referred me, and with which I was satisfied. Why was I satisfied with it? In the first place, when the compromise measures of 1850 were passed, I was not a member of the Senate. I was a member of the Cabinet when they were brought to President Fillmore. I was for their approval. Congress had determined the details; it was for the President to see whether the laws were constitutional, not whether they were good laws. It is sometimes said that Congress, by the compromises of 1850, renounced its power over the Territories.

Mr. McCLERNAND. Renounced the policy of exercising it.

Mr. CORWIN. I hold that to be a very different question. I suppose that Congress has the power to declare war against the whole world, although nobody intends to exercise it. What I speak of is the law. The gentleman will find, if he looks to the law, that Congress reserved this power. Utah and New Mexico were to report their laws to Congress. If Congress disapproved of the laws, they were to be null and void. Does that look like surrendering the legislative power of Congress over the Territories? If Congress had not even expressly reserved the power, the acts organizing those Territories, in view of the previous history of this Territorial question, could not properly receive a different construction. But the power was expressly reserved, so that there could be no mistake about it; and every law made by either of those Territories might have been vetoed by Congress. Now, I want to stand upon high authority. I was in Congress during about ten months of that debate. A certain orator, in a place I will not name, for fear I may offend the sensibilities of some gentlemen here, in speaking of the battle of Okeechobee, said:

"Gentlemen, I can say, as an ancient Greek 'poet said, *quorum pars fui.* If you have not 'had the advantages of education, (and I dare 'say many of you have not,) that means a part 'of whom I was which." [Great laughter.]

I heard all of that Senatorial debate. I certainly heard all the earnest debate—listened to it for several months. I heard the subject debated by the great men of the day—by old men and by young men too. Webster was there; Clay was there; Mr. Calhoun made a speech upon the subject also. Will you read it now? He scarcely changed his opinions after that. He said that this doctrine of the Territories having the right to make laws for themselves was absurd. Besides, said he, it is contrary to the practice of the Government from its foundation down to the present time. I do not say it is absurd, but I agree with him in the historical fact—that it is contrary to the practices of the Government. Some of my friends at the North, and some at the West, too, thought that these compromise measures of 1850 did abandon the notion that it was expedient to legislate for the Territories. I have no quarrel to make with them now on that point. I know how they treated Webster. I hope God will forgive them for that—I cannot. What were the doctrines of Clay and Webster on the subject? They repeated them over and over again. Those men understood the law of nations. They never had any dispute about them in the Senate of the United States. By the law of nations, when one sovereignty cedes a colony or country to another, with the power of the Government passing with it, all the institutions of the ceded territory not incompatible with the fundamental law of the country to which it is ceded remain just as they were at the time of the cession, until they are changed by positive legislation. Now, apply that doctrine to Mexico. Not only was there no positive law in that territory, when acquired under the treaty of Guadalupe Hidalgo, making slavery legal, but there was a positive law against its existence. Negro slavery had been abrogated by a decree of the Mexican Government, which had not been altered or changed with regard to any of the territory which we acquired. What was the effect of that?

First, then, that there was no necessity for prohibiting slavery in those new territories, because slavery never could be there until some legislative power, having authority to make the law, established it. Slavery is the offspring of local, State, or municipal law. The sovereign legislative power over the Territories being with Congress, slavery never could be established there by law till Congress had made the law, or approved the law of the Territorial Legislature establishing it. Here were two reasons. First, it never could exist without positive law; and secondly, there was a positive law forbidding it. Such were the views and reasons assigned by the eminent men of whom I speak, for not prohibiting slavery in the territory acquired from Mexico by law of Congress.

When Mr. Clay rose in his place—whose majestic form I think I now see before me—and declared that no power on earth would ever induce him to plant slavery anywhere where it did not exist; when he said this, prepared to refer all his life's history to the tribunal of posterity, and knowing that he was soon to appear before Him who knows the motives of men, all understood his principles then, and felt their truth and power. Mr. Webster had the same view of the question precisely. He repeated it over and over again, and said he would have put a restriction upon the Territory if there had been a legal necessity for it. This idea of the Constitution introducing slavery everywhere, when not forbidden by a State Constitution, had not become fashionable then. That was in 1850, and the Dred Scott decision came after that.

Mr. Clerk, I speak of the different departments of the Government with perfect respect, but I undertake to say that neither Mr. Clay nor Mr. Webster could ever have been led to believe that the Supreme Court of the United States would decide that Congress had no power to legislate over the subject of slavery in the Territories. I shall not here discuss the Dred Scott decision, for I have passed over that already.

Now, sir, in the most extreme and warmest brotherly kindness, I will show a little of the antiquities of the Democratic party. [Laughter.] I shall speak of the Democratic party of the North. *De mortuis nihil nisi bonum.* [Laughter.] A celebrated man in our country has said that that maxim ought to be changed to "*de mortuis nihil nisi verum.*" I take that proposition and adopt it. I do not mean to accuse the Democratic party of any crime, except of being once in the right, and afterwards pursuing the wrong. My colleague from the Dayton district, [Mr. VALLANDIGHAM,] in a spirit of candor, told us the other day that the Democratic party of Ohio had been wrong on this question of slavery. I wish to show that he was right in that declaration, according to his view of it, and that if he would just change that word "wrong" into "right," the Democratic party were right according to the doctrines of the fathers of the Government; but they wandered away from the institutions of Moses, to the worship of Astheroth and other diabolical divinities. I will quote a little of their gospel, from cathedral authority, in the State of Ohio, in the year 1848, whereby I wish to show to the Democratic party of the South, as it is called, how great an act they have achieved in having converted the most hardened and abominable sinners who have existed in the world. [Laughter.]

Democratic gentlemen from the South must summon their Christian charity to this work. They must remember that our Democratic Sauls of Tarsus were on the way to Damascus in 1848, bent upon persecuting Democratic Christians in the South. You see how they divided the clothes of the Southern Stephen, and stoned him to death. You will rejoice, however, to see how "a great light shone upon them" in 1854, and how they heard about that time a voice from the South, and lo! upon the instant, they donned their "sandal shoon and scallop shell," and, with meek submission and pious zeal, they made their pilgrimage from the icy regions of old constitutional faith to the sunny realms of Southern novelties, where, to this day, they remain in "brotherly love." Miracles had not ceased! But who shall say whether these wanderers from their old homes may not grow weary of their new abodes, and yet turn their faces to Judea, crying, "When I forget thee, O Jerusalem, may my right hand forget its cunning!" But let me refer you to their heresies; but be not alarmed, for they are all safe now:

"*Resolved*, That the people of Ohio now, as 'they have always done, looking upon the institution of slavery as an evil, unfavorable to the 'full development of our institutions"—

These Democratic people have had greatly at heart *that* "development of our institutions." They were speaking for the people of the State of Ohio—for the Whigs held the same ideas exactly, with one exception, which I shall state directly—

—"unfavorable to the full development of our in'stitutions; and that, entertaining these senti'ments, they will feel it to be their duty to use all 'the powers consistent with the national compact 'to prevent its increase, to mitigate, [here is the 'point on which I differ with them,] *and finally 'eradicate it.*"

The classical mind of my colleague from the Dayton district suggests to him the etymological meaning of that horrible word [laughter] "eradicate"—not lop it off, not prevent its growing into other fields from those in which it is now planted; but to walk into the South, and take slavery there, and grub it up—provided the Constitution will allow it. What do you charge these SEWARD men with? You say that they will act according to the forms of the Constitution; that they will get an overruling power in the popular department of the Government—in this House; that they will get a majority of the Senate; that they will have a willing, obedient Executive in the White House; and then, that they will walk over the Constitution. That is precisely what the Democratic party of Ohio proposed to do. We Whigs never did propose to do that. We never believed that we had any business to "eradicate" slavery. We never intimated that we could interfere with it in the South, or that we desired to interfere with it. But your Democratic brethren, with whom you are now associating so happily, believed that identical doctrine. You charge Mr. SEWARD with having introduced into the brain of John Brown the idea that slavery ought to be uprooted in the States. I suppose he had seen this resolution passed by the great Democratic party of Ohio in 1848. I think he lived in that State. You have been spending days and weeks—seven weeks—in proving that John Brown never would have been at Harper's Ferry, and that Helper never would have written his book—although he wrote it two or three years before Mr. SEWARD made the remark—if they had not heard that WILLIAM H. SEWARD said there was "an irrepressible conflict" between free labor and slave labor. That is altogether too philosophical an idea for an enthusiast like John Brown to take hold of. He had been reading the Old Testament. He was a member of the old New England school of Presbyterians. He believed it was his duty to draw the sword of the Lord and Gideon, and to smite the heathen, everywhere he could, with sword and battle-ax—not with argument. That is the way with that set of people. In every battle-field of the Revolution, if these Yankee regiments were there, and had the slightest chance before the encounter with the British foe, they would kneel down and invoke the aid of that God who of old had bared His right arm for the salvation of his people. These were the kind of men from whom John Brown sprang. When he saw the great State of Ohio represented by the Democratic party, and heard them say that slavery was an enormous evil — an evil which prevented the development of the glorious institutions for which his fathers had fought, what would be his reflection? "What is to be done to eradicate this institution?" He would say: "I will strike at this unholy thing that im-'pedes the onward march of this Government 'to that consummation which shall give freedom 'to all men!"

Mr. VALLANDIGHAM. The other part of the resolution has not been read. As there are some peculiar beauties in it, illustrative of the first part, I regret that my distinguished colleague has been so unfortunate as not to have it in his possession.

Mr. CORWIN. That is the whole of one resolution. The next resolution reads:

"*But be it further resolved*, That the Democracy 'of Ohio do, at the same time, fully recognise 'the doctrine held by the early fathers of the 'Republic, and still maintained by the Demo-'cratic party in all the States, that to each State 'belongs the right to adopt and modify its own 'municipal laws; to regulate its own internal 'affairs; to hold and maintain an equal and in-'dependent sovereignty with each and every 'other State; and that upon these rights the Na-'tional Legislature can neither legislate nor en-'croach."

That is an entirely different thing. What the Democratic party proposed to do was to eradicate slavery by some means or other. The great sin that the Republican party has committed is, it holds at this day the doctrine which the Democratic party announced in 1848, though it does not pretend, and has never pretended, that slavery should be eradicated in the States, otherwise than by the States themselves.

I will cheerfully read the resolutions of the Ohio Democracy in 1840, to which my colleague refers. Here they are:

"*Resolved*, That, in the opinion of this Con-'vention, Congress ought not, without the con-'sent of the people of the District, and of the 'States of Virginia and Maryland, to abolish 'slavery in the District of Columbia; and that 'the efforts now making for that purpose, by 'organized societies in the free States, are hos-'tile to the spirit of the Constitution, and de-'structive to the harmony of the Union.

"*Resolved*, That slavery, being a domestic in-'stitution recognised by the Constitution of the 'United States, we, as citizens of a free State, 'have no right to interfere with it; and that the 'organizing of societies and associations in the 'free States, in opposition to the institutions of 'sister States, while productive of no good, may 'be the cause of much mischief; and while such 'associations, for political purposes, ought to be 'discountenanced by every lover of peace and 'concord, no sound Democrat will have part or 'lot with them.

"*Resolved*, That political Abolitionism is but 'ancient Federalism, under a new guise; and 'that the political action of anti-slavery societies 'is only a device for the overthrow of Democ-'racy."

Now, Mr. Clerk, it becomes me, of course, to make some remarks. They had abolition societies springing up in those days, and at that time it was doubtful with which party these Abolitionists would vote. They put up a separate ticket, and it was this very ticket that elected a President of the United States in 1844, and changed the history and destiny of this Republic. Gentlemen remind me that Governor Chase, of Ohio, is a good Republican now, and a member of the Republican party, and was a member of the Liberty party in 1844. I believe all this is true. Governor Chase's principles are now well known. He is a Republican now; nothing more. All men who believe, as the Abolitionists say they believe, that slavery is such an inherent wrong that the Constitution and laws can give it no validity, will go with the Republican party for restricting it in any place where it does not exist, though it is now a fact that Abolitionists, as a party, will have no affiliation with the Republicans. While, at the same time, this Abolition Society, which always was opposed to the Whig party, because they did not go far enough upon this subject, defeated Henry Clay, the great Whig champion, made Mr. Polk President, acquired territory, and brought upon you the very questions which are now before you.

What I mean to say, sir, is, that in 1848 the Northern Democratic party held these doctrines, going further than the Whig party of that day, reaching out their arms further to get hold of slavery in the States—for I conceive their action means nothing else—in some form, by public opinion, or in some other way, to restrict it, and finally to eradicate it. Well, they went on their way rejoicing. But in 1848, it may be remembered, the Democratic party was carried captive to Babylon; Zachary Taylor was elected President, and he was a Whig. The Democracy hung their harps upon the willows, by the streams of Babylon, and lifted up their voices and wept, [laughter,] and mourned over the slain of the daughters of their people. What then happened? Why, we maintained the doctrine that you may restrict slavery; we stood with the fathers, the courts, the Congresses, and the Presidents, in an unbroken and unobstructed current of authority, up to the year 1852. The Democrats of the North woke up suddenly, and said that slavery was a very good thing—that it helped to develop the resources of the country, and improved it.

I only want to show that the Republicans cannot be converted as quickly as the Democrats. I only want to show that we are somewhat obstinate in our old opinions, and that when we go back, and get into the assemblies of the Fathers—old men whose garments were yet wet with the waters of the Red Sea through which they had passed for our deliverance—we find that they held the Republican doctrines with respect to the Territories. We cannot account for the sudden conversion of our Democratic brethren of the North. I hope they are happy in their new faith. I want all men to be happy, all people to be happy—men, women, and children. I see that, they are happy. For instance, if the gentleman from Georgia [Mr. CRAWFORD] were to get into a loving mood with the Democracy of the North, he might murmur in the ear of my colleague [Mr. VALLANDIGHAM] a verse from the elegies of Shenstone:

> "Dear region of silence and shade,"

in reference to the Democratic party, [laughter;] and then Mr. VALLANDIGHAM, in his softest notes of affection, would take up the strain—

> "Soft scenes of contentment and ease,
> Where I have so happily strayed,
> Since naught in thy absence could please."

Now, it is pleasant to see them thus dwelling together; for it is impossible for such a man as I am, much as I am opposed to their doctrines, to fail to sympathize with men, when I see they are perfectly happy. Long may they live; long may they live; for if they were to die suddenly, they might die in their sins. [Great laughter.]

A very curious question is this thing of life, and what a man may do in a lifetime. In 1848, the Democratic party, with their eyeballs bloodshot, and the perspiration dropping off their noses, like one of our sugar-trees in February, upon the south side of a hill, [loud laughter,] with their resolution in one hand, and the torch of abolition philosophy in the other, marched through the country, proclaiming universal liberty, and the final advent of that day when slavery should be no longer recognised in the land. That is what they did in eight short years—between 1848 and 1856. That is but a short time in the annals of this country. Suppose any man had been gifted as it is supposed the Wandering Jew was; suppose Adam had been cursed with a continued existence up to this day, and had started off with this doctrine in the beginning, and had changed every eight years, how many times would *he* have changed? [Laughter.] Threescore and ten years seem to be the allotted period of man in this age of the world; and in that time he might change seven or eight times. Now, my Republican friends, do not be discouraged. My Democratic friends upon the other side of the House, do not let me make you unhappy. This is the year before the Presidential election. Do not flatter yourselves that your Church is well founded, and that you can go through another Presidential election as you went through the last. Besides, man is given to change; mutability is stamped on all things. "Man is of few days and full of sorrow," [laughter,] "he cometh forth like a flower, is cut down, and fleeth away like a shadow"—every eight years. [Roars of laughter.]

In 1850 the present fugitive slave law was passed. Now, it is always necessary, in order to understand the gyrations of political parties, to know what happened accidentally or incidentally about a particular time. A gentleman, who had been judge of our Supreme Court of Ohio, was a Democratic candidate for Governor of Ohio in 1852. Mr. Fillmore was then President, and his was called a Whig Administration. The extreme anti-slavery people of the State of Ohio did not like him. They abhorred him. Mr. Fillmore was President at the time of the passage of these compromise measures. What had the Democratic party to complain of in them? Nothing. The fugitive slave law had been passed, and Mr. Fillmore had given it his approval. Judge Wood, the candidate of the Democratic party, which had a great majority in Ohio, was elected Governor of the State, and in his message to the Legislature he said:

"While public opinion may be divided, per-'haps, on the law, [the fugitive slave bill,] there 'is, nevertheless, another matter in close con-'nection with it, on which it is believed the 'sentiments of the people are entirely united. 'The area of slavery must never be extended in 'this Government while the voice, the united 'voice, and action of Ohio, in any constitutional 'form, can stay it. Here, with propriety, we may 'take our stand. Thus far, proud wave, shalt 'thou advance, but no further shalt thou come."

What did that mean? You shall never have

another slave State in the Union. You shall never establish slavery in another Territory of the United States. The political voice of the Democratic party of Ohio had spoken in that language in 1848. In 1852, the embodiment of it in the gubernatorial office of that State proclaimed the sentiments that I have read. I do not say now that Governor Wood was wrong, or that the Democratic party was wrong; but I only say that mutability is stamped on all human things.

Now, I ask, how can the Democratic people of the North sit still and hear the Republican party denounced as disorganizers and disunionists, and as disloyal to the Constitution, as they are denounced every hour and every day? The accusing eloquence of these Southern men has been brought in full volume of rich rhetoric, and launched on the heads of the Republican party, while, as I have shown, they have only followed in the footsteps of the Northern Democrats. The only difference is, that, as we think we have derived our principles from the founders of the Republic, and as our doctrines are sanctified by executive and judicial and legislative approbation, we choose rather to follow these old principles than to take up with new-fangled doctrines. Can you not forgive us for that? If we be mistaken, can you not suppose that, at least, we think we are doing right? Do you suppose we ever intend to go into your States, and interfere with you there? There is not a man of you who can delude himself into the belief that we have any idea of subverting this glorious Union, which we worship so much that we believe every word and every syllable of the fathers' sayings. Now, I wish to announce that the day has gone by that these things will be heard without response. This question shall be tried here, if we can ever organize. Then it shall be brought to the standard of constitutional law, on canons of construction that have been admitted ever since the intellect of man operated on the construction of language; and we will try conclusions with the gentlemen of the South. Moreover, if you announce, as you have done, that this Union shall be dissolved, that this constitutional Confederacy of ours shall be broken up, because the people of the North choose to elect a President—a man whom you do not like—we shall see where the treason really lies.

That is my view of the subject. I think I am the most placable man that was ever born of woman. I am prepared to enter into this controversy with gentlemen like brethren—to controvert these matters as statesmen, if we can elevate ourselves to that position, and submit to a candid world to decide who is right. If the world decide against us, depend upon it that we shall believe we have misapprehended the public opinion of the country, and shall submit to whatever award that public opinion may make. That, in this country, is the final arbiter of all controversies of this kind, and must be obeyed. In the mean time, I warn Democratic gentlemen to remember that a doctrine is now coming up from the South, that the inhabitants of a Territory have no power to prohibit slavery therein. Parties have so divided the people of the country, that they have begun to consider themselves enemies; and we, instead of considering ourselves the "conscript fathers" of the people, bound to consider the interests, not of one State, but of all the States, have commenced to regard ourselves as the diplomatic Representatives of particular sections of the country. I hold that every man on this floor is the Representative of every man, woman, and child, in the Republic; and every act which he does, in a national aspect, must operate for good or for evil on all. I hold that a man who acts for his section, and not for the Union, does not comprehend the great duty that he is sent here to discharge. Our fathers intended that Representatives should be elected by districts, because then they would be well known to the electors; but they meant that when here, and after they had taken the oath, they should be just as much the Representatives of every district in the United States as of the district that sent them. That is my conception of our duty. That, I know, was the idea of the fathers who made the Republic, and formed the House as it is now formed.

Suppose us assembled together, Mr. Clerk, with these feelings, and called on to legislate for the Territories that belong to us all—that were won by the common blood and common treasure of all; what would we then say? We would say this: "There are certain portions of our 'children in the South who have property which 'will not prove of any worth to them in the cold 'latitudes of this Territory. They cannot go 'there. There are certain other children of this 'family of ours—poor people, as we call them, 'meaning those who must work for their living—'and I hope that men will always be compelled to 'work in some way, with the head or hand, for 'an honest living—and here is the territory 'lying beyond the Mississippi, called Kansas and 'Nebraska, for which Congress has power to 'make all needful rules and regulations; let 'them go there." In the Territories are emigrants from the State of Georgia, from Virginia, from all the States of the East and the West. Your own constituents are the relations and dear friends of these people. So are mine. They are unacquainted with each other; a heterogeneous people, not yet homogeneous enough to make their own laws in harmony.

When we prohibit slavery in a Territory, we allow men from all the States to go there with the same rights exactly. While a man from a slave State may not take a slave into the Territory and hold him in slavery, neither can one of my children in Ohio purchase a negro in Kentucky and take him there, and hold him as a slave. Is not that equally just to all? I know that you say every one should go there with his property, of whatever kind; but I say that this law of inhibiting slavery is equal and just to men of every section. Everybody may go there with the same sort of property. We make no distinction between any. If it be a Territory in which slave labor is unprofitable, you ought to be rebuked, from the mere motive of economy. Let us look at it as a mere question of economy.

The whole country belongs to us, and you are our children. We are to divide it among you. Suppose you have one son who can work in a warm climate, and another who can work in a cold climate. In dividing your estate between them, you give to each that portion of it which suits his wants in that respect. You have one a mechanic; you do not give him a farm, and set him to work as a farmer. Neither should you take the negro to work where his labor would be unprofitable.

Mr. REAGAN. I understand the gentleman is now speaking for the Republican party.

Mr. CORWIN. No, sir; I am speaking for a leader of that party. [Laughter.]

Mr. REAGAN. Then I ask the gentleman for himself, and not for the Republican party, if he recognises the right of people owning slaves to go into a Territory in a Southern latitude, and occupy that Territory with their slaves with the protection of the Government?

Mr. CORWIN. I will speak for myself. If you acquire territory by treaty, and the people in it hold slaves, I would not, against their will, interfere with slavery *there.* I would act, in that particular, just as the Congresses of 1798 and 1804 acted in relation to Mississippi and Orleans Territories. If slavery were there, I would not disturb it. I would not interfere with the rights of property against the will of the people; and if you get territory where the white man cannot work, I would permit people of the States to send their slaves there; and when there, certainly, I would protect them, if protection were wanted. I agree with the gentlemen of the extreme South in one point: whenever you can show me that, under the laws and Constitution of the United States, (as you phrase it, under the Constitution,) slavery is lawfully in a Territory, I hold it to be a duty to make laws to protect property *lawfully* held anywhere, if such laws be necessary for its protection; but remember, I do not believe that the Constitution takes slavery into Territories, or anywhere else. Slavery is the creature of local, municipal law. Whenever you acquire a territory where slavery exists, if you have a treaty sanctioned by two-thirds of the Senate of the United States, you are just as sure of slavery as we are sure of what we call "freedom" in Ohio. I dare say that some of my tender-footed brethren on the Republican side of the House wince a little at that, but I act upon possibilities and upon probabilities.

And there is another thing which you do, which is totally at war with one of the fundamental maxims of our Government. You begin by sending forth to the world the very doctrines of Rousseau's social compact—that Government claims its rightful authority from the consent of the people governed. And then you conquer a country, and a part is ceded to you, but no consent of the people thus ceded is ever asked. You seize them and govern them, whether they consent or not. You did not ask the people of California or New Mexico whether they were willing to be American citizens. You took the treaty, and you took the lands and the people. So when you get Cuba—which you will not get soon; but whenever you do get it, if you ever should, slavery will be there; and the Spanish Government, when it cedes that island, will say that you shall take the people, with all their rights of property. That is sure to be done, if the time ever arrives when you are to acquire Cuba. So if you acquire territory where white men cannot work. There are such countries; I have been told so by the best physicians I ever knew. What do you want with such territory, unless you have slaves, if it be true that free negroes will not work without coercion? If I were the father of all the world, and I had some children who could work in cold and temperate climates, I would send them there to work; and if I had other children who could work only in the warmer portions of the globe, I would send them there; and if they would not go, I would make them. I am not speaking of constitutional law. I look at society as it is. What will you do with the men who will not work, and will eat? I know what we do with them in Ohio. We send them to the poor-house, and make them work. Some, for reasons known to the law, are sent to the penitentiary, where they are deprived of their *inalienable right* to liberty. That is a question we cannot discuss here. I state it for the benefit of weak brothers, who never think about the matter. [Laughter.] If my white son would not work in the proper place for him, I would punish him; and if I had a black man, who, like the anaconda, fattened upon malaria, and only lived well in a rice swamp, there I would make him go.

I know that I have no right to do anything of that kind. The moral right, according to our conceptions of God's will, meets with a different interpretation in the different countries of the world. One of the most honest, upright men of all the Roman Emperors I ever read of—I mean Vespasian—took thirty thousand Jewish prisoners when he went to conquer Judea. He pledged the honor of a Roman general, that, if these men surrendered, they should receive quarter and be treated as prisoners of war. When he came to hold a council of war as to what disposition should be made of them, every officer was for killing them. They said, "If the Emperor trust them upon parole of honor, there is no faith in the Jews, and to-morrow they will be killing us." The question put was like the celebrated speech of a Scotch colonel, in the army of Gustavus Adolphus. The commander-in-chief, before a certain engagement, ordered that each one of his colonels should make a speech at the head of his regiment. The old Scotchman, who had never done anything in his life but cleave skulls, said: "My lads, ye see those fellows in black. Well, if ye dinna kill them, they maun kill you." That was a difficult question to be decided by Vespasian's council of war. How was it compromised? The honor of a Roman general was pledged. (So is mine. I am sworn to obey the Constitution and the laws of the country.) It was agreed that one portion of the prisoners should be spared and treated as prisoners of war, that another should be sold into slavery, and the remainder put to death. Alas! for poor human nature.

We will always kill a man when we know he is going to kill us. It seems, then, that having no such power as I have stated, nations, like families, must let each other alone.

The slave trade, as I have said already, was an abomination from the beginning. It was wrong in the beginning. Year after year I have listened to talk, on one side and on the other, about this question of negro slavery. I was a delegate to the Colonization Society, which met at the Smithsonian Institution. I thought I would go there, and see whether I could hear a solution of this question. One of the most eloquent and learned men I have listened to for a long time, made an address. He was one of those divines who, I know, will preach what he believes. He said that the finger of God was plainly to be seen in the slave trade. In old times, Governor Oglethorpe endeavored to keep slavery out of Georgia, as every man knows who has read the history of that State. It was brought there, and he could not keep it out. Whitfield, that eminent divine, was there. He told Oglethorpe to let slavery alone, for the hand of the Almighty was in it. He said, "we have been 'trying to Christianize the world; we are at it 'now; and what progress have our missionaries 'made? Very little, or none. Let the poor negro 'be brought into this country, and whether his 'master likes it or not, he will imbibe some idea 'of the morals of Christianity, and in due time 'the right missionaries will be those of the black 'race, to return among their own color. Thus, 'that wicked man who sold this people into sla-'very, in the hands of Heaven will have proved 'the instrument of bringing them to Christianity 'and civilization."

If the finger of God be in slavery, let the Southern man take care how he treats these missionaries, these instruments of Heaven for the great work of Christianizing the heathen African. Keep them in slavery if you will; but, as that Whitfield said, you cannot take a negro and keep him ten years in this country, without his becoming a more enlightened man than when he left the shores of Africa. Take care that you give him freely that light. The present generation of negroes, sprung from those brought here a century ago, will, I believe, compare favorably with the most intelligent of their own countrymen in Africa. Let us, then, not despair of the ultimate fortunes of the negro races. We hear of what is doing in Liberia. I must remind my boastful white brethren here, that the history of the legislation in *that* black colony would warrant any one in the conclusion that our colored brethren there would have organized their Congress with more temperate judgment, and in much shorter time, than we have consumed in our efforts, which, up to this time, seem to promise no very speedy result. [Laughter.]

Who knows, sir, but that slavery may accomplish the great work of Christianizing and civilizing the African race? May we not hope, that while these people are content, even in slavery, to advance in civilization in this country, and to develop the resources of countries which it is said can be developed by slave labor alone, the great ends and purposes of Him who sits enthroned in the circle of the heavens will be accomplished by some agency to us as yet unknown.

That wonderful man, Cyrus, did not know that he was executing the commands of God, when he invaded Babylon, as it had been foretold. So it may be that you, who so much admire the institution of slavery—and I do not mean to discuss its merits here—like Cyrus, may be the chosen instruments, even against your own wishes, to work out the purposes of Almighty God. When your negroes shall have reached the point of civilization which will fit them to enjoy that portion of liberty which a rational Government may give them, then they will no longer be your slaves. They will then stay and work with you for moderate wages, cheaper than the white man can, or they will go abroad, such of them as choose to go, on the great errand of the great Master of us all, to carry the light of His Gospel to a benighted people. I think that looks plausible enough. Nothing in this debate has given me so much pleasure as listening to the gentleman from Louisiana, [Mr. Davidson,] when he told us upon this side of the House, that the Gospel is preached upon his plantation in Louisiana, just as it is preached in the churches in the North. And so Southern members assure me it is everywhere in the South. When the master conducts himself in that way to his poor, ignorant slave, he will be enlightened.

If it be possible for the black man—and that is a question upon which I am no philosopher—to rise by slow and gradual degrees to that intellectual and moral eminence which shall qualify him for another state than that which he now occupies, depend upon it, masters, when the time comes, will be willing to assent to the change of his condition. So I think slavery, so I think history, teaches us. But in the mean time I admit that there are a great many evils connected with the system.

I assure gentlemen of the South that that kind of discipline which our education and mode of life at the North give us does not allow us to be quite so free in the indulgence of these fits of ill temper which come upon us at times, whether in the North or South, or in the expression which may be given in words to that frailty. You are good and honorable gentlemen, but you make entirely too much noise for our Northern tastes, [laughter,] and you are "too sudden and quick in quarrel." But do not misunderstand the people of the North. Their education and training teach them to govern their passions. That is just the difference between us. But when the quarrel does come, which to them appears just, why, then I will not enter into recognizance that they will keep the peace. I have seen it tried before now.

Why, then, shall we not have harmony? I assert here—and I care not for anybody's criticism—that this slavery question would not exist two hours in this House, if you passed a resolution not to acquire any more territory for ten years. If it could be that there should not be another Presidential election for ten years, that of itself would bring peace. The cause of discontent and strife, in a great measure, is, that we must have a Presidential election in a few months. You do not want any more slave territory. How will you fill up Texas, which has been generously devoted for all the surplus slaves for fifty years? Do you expect to find a milder climate or a better latitude? You quarrel with the people of the North about the settlement of Kansas. There are four States for you to fill, where you can go unquestioned. Go first and bring into cultivation those fertile lands yet unoccupied, before you think of another expansion of territory. You will not go there, but stand here quarrelling with us, Northern Republicans, because you cannot get more territory. If you had more territory, you could not settle it, because you have not the slave labor.

A gentleman upon the other side of the House called out to us the other day: "Disband your Republican party; disband it; you threaten the peace of the Union." Sir, I am not afraid of this Union. I see plainly enough that I can save it in the last extremity, just by letting a Democrat be elected President. [Great laughter.] Ever since I found that out, I have cared little what you say about danger to the Union. The gentleman from Mississippi [Mr. BARKSDALE] declared, also, that his State would go right off out of the Union, in the event of the election of Mr. SEWARD. The people of the State of Mississippi may walk out, but the State never will. Why, sir, I have heard of this thing ever since I have heard anything in public affairs. In 1833, South Carolina was determined to go out of the Union, because of what she deemed an excessive duty on foreign goods. Pennsylvania was going out because we taxed her whisky in 1794; and Massachusetts thought the Union was endangered when Louisiana was purchased. Each and all of these States yet remain, and are, I trust, loyal to the Union. I have lived through three dissolutions of the Union myself, [great laughter,] and the Union is stronger to-day than when its dissolution was first threatened—stronger than it was in the beginning. The State of Mississippi is a glorious little State, covered all over with cotton; and, in my judgment, she will be "cotton to" the Union to the last. [Laughter.] All these planets which revolve around this great constitutional centre, whence truth, light, political knowledge radiate, may threaten to fly off occasionally. Mississippi may seem to fly off in some eccentric orbit, but she will soon return to her proper perihelion. I do not say how she will do it, but she certainly will do it of her own accord. Let us then hear no more of this angry talk about disunion; but, like men, like brethren, as we are, work earnestly and happily together for the common good of all.

As to this question of Territorial legislation, touching slavery in the Territories, let gentlemen pause upon that, and consider before they rush to conclusions. I tell gentlemen of the South—and the day will come when they will remember my advice—not to trust Northern people to make laws of their own in the Territories for the exclusion or protection of slavery. I do not care where you go, in any latitute under the heavens where a white man can live and work, the Yankees will go there too. Wherever clocks can be used or sold, there they will be. If they come to learn that it is the law of the Republic that the *status* of the country is fixed forever by the first inhabitants, instead of settling that *status* here, among men who are responsible to the country and to history, they will settle the question as they did in Kansas. They will always beat you, if you open the question in that way. Let this calm, deliberate, legislative assembly of gentlemen, who legislate for the whole Union of thirty millions of people—let them determine whether it is better that slavery should go there or not; let that question come here, where we look at this great country, and all the Territories we have, and all we may ever acquire, as common patrimony, alike of all the States, and all the people we represent.

The population which usually goes into new Territories is generally led by an eager and sometimes wild spirit of adventure. The people will keep out the negro, because they have no negroes of their own, no slaves of their own. I care not whether the Territory be at the north pole or near the equator, they will go there, and will keep your negroes out, if you allow them to determine whether slavery shall be there or not. I should think that any man who has looked at the history of Kansas for the last three years, with reference to this matter, will not doubt my conclusions. In consequence of Congress giving up this great conservative power to make laws for an uncongenial, heterogeneous people, civil war raged for three years over the beautiful plains of Kansas, where there should have been nothing heard but the jocund whistle of the plowman driving his team to the field, and where nothing else or worse would have been heard, if Congress had only made laws to govern that Territory, and sent its Governor, and, if necessary, troops, to execute the law. You made an experiment there, and you know the result.

What have you in another Territory now? You say you cannot make laws for Utah. You have denied the power of Congress to make laws for the Territories. What is Utah? A blot on the fair pages of your history, which all the waters of Lethe can never wash out—a foul, incestuous den of miserable adulterers and murderers—a disgrace to a civilized and Chistian country. That is what comes of this glorious new doctrine which you have propagated on all sides. That comes of your parting with the wise usages and the wise institutions of your fathers; and so it will ever be, the moment you abandon those well-established, constitutional rules fixed by the founders of the Republic. You have abandoned the great highways of the past—the good macadamized roads made for you—every milestone of which was red with revolutionary blood; you have strayed away from them, and wandered after wills-o'-the-wisp into swamps and by-paths. All that the Republican party wish to do, is to stand up and call you back as a mother calls to her lost child, and put you on the safe old road again. They call upon you to come out of the wilderness; to quit the shedding of each others' blood in fratricidal war for the right to have this or that law; to let the Congress of the United States, who represent the fathers, the brothers, the sisters, of the peaceful emigrants who have gone into the Territories, consider what is best for their children and friends. But abandon, as you have abandoned, the institutions of your Fathers, and there will be neither peace nor progress in the Territories. There will be strife here, and civil war there, and wild confusion will reign supreme.

The wise prophet of Israel, after he came down from the mountain with the law in his hand, and found his brother Aaron worshipping a golden calf which he had made, was so angry that he threw down the tables of the law, and broke them. He determined that that wicked people should never have an opportunity of worshipping any more golden calves: he made all the women bring in their trinkets and golden ornaments, and melted them down in one mass. Let us, in the same spirit, bring in these miserable idols of ours; sacrifice them on the common altar of our country; shake hands, forget, and forgive.

And now, before I sit down, let me ask again, are the destinies of this mighty Republic to turn on the publication of a pamphlet? You know that the gentleman whom we have nominated will make a just and impartial Speaker. Concede that for once. Concede that we will have to elect by a plurality. I think that, if we could, we ought to elect by a majority. There is something symmetrical in it. You say, he should be elected by a majority, because, in the happening of two or three very remote contingencies, he may become President of the United States. But, as I said yesterday, no President or Vice President will ever be found, both amiable enough to die and let the Speaker take that place. We will not consider that contingency. If we cannot agree upon one man, is it possible, in the name of the American people, that we cannot find some man in this Congress who is fit to preside over this House?

It has been stated that I said that I would vote for Mr. SHERMAN till the last trump should sound. A better man than I am changed his mind. David, King of Israel, repented of what he said, when he remarked, "I have said, in my haste, that all men are liars." I concede that fact, when I state now that I am willing to vote for any one almost who can be elected. If this protracted contest mean anything, we cannot elect a Republican; we cannot elect a Lecompton Democrat; we cannot elect an anti-Lecompton Democrat; and though there may be as many shades of party as Jacob had stripes in his cattle—I do not know how many—it seems that we cannot elect any one of them. I know of but one man in this House who does not belong to any party, and I have thought that perhaps we might unite upon him. The gentleman from New York [Mr. HORACE F. CLARK] belongs to no party; he will not act with any party; does not love any party; does not hate any party; does not care for any party. [Great laughter.] Why not elect him?

Mr. Clerk, I believe that I am abusing my privileges here. [Cries of "Go on!"]

I hope the observations which I have made, Mr. Clerk, forced from me without any of that preparation which is usual, may not be entirely worthless. Whether we consider this ever-recurring question of slavery as resting within our unrestricted discretion, or whether we regard it as fixed and limited by constitutional law—in either aspect, with good sense, guided by true patriotism—there is nothing to be feared. The way through the future is, in my judgment, open, clear, and plain. We cannot be so weak as to give way to childish fears, or sink into lethargy and despair. On the contrary, let us "gird up our loins" to the work before us; for upon us this duty is devolved. We cannot escape from it, if we would. Let us, above all, preserve our Constitution inviolate, and the Union which it created unbroken. By the lights they give us, with the aids of an enlightened religion, and an ever-improving Christian philosophy, let us march onward and onward in the great highway of social progress. Let us always keep in the advancing car of that progress—our book of Constitutions, and our Bible. Like the Jews of old, let the ark of the covenant be advanced to the front in our march. With these to guide us, I feel the proud assurance that our free principles will take their way through all coming time; and before them I do believe that the cloven-footed altars of oppression, all over the world, will fall down, as Dagon of old fell down, and was shivered to pieces in the presence of the ark of the living God.

But if we halt in this great exodus of the nations; if we are broken into inconsiderable fragments, and ultimately dispersed, through our follies of this day, what imagination can compass the frightful enormity of our crime! What would the world say of this unpardonable sin? Rather than this, we should pray the kind Father of all, even His wicked children, to visit us with the last and worst of all the afflictions that fall on sin and sinful man. Better for us would it be that the fruitful earth should be smitten for a season with barrenness, and become dry dust, and refuse its annual fruits; better that the heavens for a time should become brass, and the ear of God deaf to our prayers; better that Famine, with her cold and skinny fingers, should lay hold upon the throats of our wives and children; better that God should commission the Angel of Destruction to go forth over the land, scattering pestilence and death from his dusky wing, than that we should prove faithless to our trust, and by that means our light should be quenched, our liberties destroyed, and all our bright hopes die out in that night which knows no coming dawn.

Note.—This pamphlet edition of Mr. CORWIN's speech is published by a committee, who, with a view to put it in the most compact form, have omitted all of the *Globe's* report which it was possible to omit. Hence the most of the colloquies with gentlemen who interrupted Mr. CORWIN, in the course of his remarks, are excluded.

WASHINGTON, D. C.
BUELL & BLANCHARD, PRINTERS.
Stereotyped by Blanchard's Process, Patented February 22, 1859.
C. W. MURRAY, STEREOTYPER.
1860.

PRESIDENTIAL CAMPAIGN OF 1860.

REPUBLICAN EXECUTIVE CONGRESSIONAL COMMITTEE.

HON. PRESTON KING, N. Y., *Chairman.*
" J. W. GRIMES, IOWA.
" L. F. S. FOSTER, CONN.
On the part of the Senate.
" E. B. WASHBURNE, ILLINOIS.

HON. JOHN COVODE, PENN., *Treasurer.*
" E. G. SPAULDING, N. Y.
" J. B. ALLEY, MASS.
" DAVID KILGORE, INDIANA.
" J. L. N. STRATTON, N. J.
On the part of the House of Reps.

The Committee are prepared to furnish the following speeches:

EIGHT PAGES.

Hon. W. H. Seward, N. Y.: State of the Country.
" W. H. Seward, N. Y.: Rochester Speech.
" G. A. Grow, Penn.: Free Homes for Free Men.
" James Harlan, Iowa: Shall the Territories be Africanized?
" John Hickman, Penn.: Who have Violated Compromises.
" B. F. Wade, Ohio: Invasion of Harper's Ferry.
" G. W. Scranton and J. H. Campbell, Penn.: The Speakership.
" F. P. Blair, Mo., Address at Cincinnati: Colonization and Commerce.
" Orris S. Ferry, Conn.
" William Windom, Minn.: The Homestead Bill—Its Friends and its Foes.
Lands for the Landless—A Tract.

SIXTEEN PAGES.

Hon. Lyman Trumbull, Ill.: Seizure of the Arsenals at Harper's Ferry, Va. and Liberty, Mo., and in Vindication of the Republican Party.
" B. F. Wade, Ohio: Property in the Territories.
" C. H. Van Wyck, N. Y.: True Democracy—History Vindicated.
" J. J. Perry, Me.: "Posting the Books between the North and the South."
" J. R. Doolittle, Wis.: The Calhoun Revolution—Its Basis and its Progress.
Hon. H. Wilson, Mass.: Territorial Slave Code.
" John P. Hale, N. H.
" Abraham Lincoln, Ill.: The Demands of the South—The Republican Party Vindicated.
Carl Schurz, Wis.: Douglas and Popular Sovereignty.

TWENTY-FOUR PAGES.

Hon. Jacob Collamer, Vermont.

THIRTY-TWO PAGES.

Hon. Thomas Corwin, of Ohio.

GERMAN.

EIGHT PAGES.

Hon. G. A. Grow, Penn.: Free Homes for Free Men.
" James Harlan, Iowa: Shall the Territories be Africanized?
" John Hickman, Penn.: Who Have Violated Compromises.
Carl Schurz, Wis.: Douglas and Popular Sovereignty.

SIXTEEN PAGES.

Hon. Lyman Trumbull, Ill.: Seizure of the Arsenals at Harper's Ferry, Va. and Liberty, Mo., and in Vindication of the Republican Party.
" W. H. Seward, N. Y.: The State of the Country.
Lands for the Landless—A Tract.

During the Presidential Campaign, Speeches and Documents will be supplied at the following reduced prices:

Eight pages, per hundred, copies free of postage,	- - - - - -	$0.50
Sixteen " " " "	- - - - - -	1.00
Twenty-four " " " "	- - - - - -	1.50

Address either of the above Committee.

GEORGE HARRINGTON, *Secretary*

www.ingramcontent.com/pod-product-compliance
Lightning Source LLC
LaVergne TN
LVHW011133110826
845150LV00008B/2322
9781418194093